EXPAT WIFE

HAPPY LIFE!

THE JOURNEY OF A **SERIAL EXPAT**

Florence Reisch-Gentinetta

Expat Wife, Happy Life!
The journey of a serial expat

First published in 2021 by

Panoma Press Ltd
48 St Vincent Drive, St Albans, Herts, AL1 5SJ, UK
info@panomapress.com
www.panomapress.com

Book layout by Neil Coe.

978-1-784529-56-7

DEDICATION

To my husband Alexander and my children
Constantin and Angelina

I love you and let's keep "living the life!"

PRAISE FOR THIS BOOK

"Very intimate, you feel the author as a friend talking to you! A friend brimming with positive energy and great wisdom. The book covers both the psychological and the practical aspects of expatriation. It is a very rich book – read it in one morning!! – that resonated in me and enlightened aspects of expatriation that I was not even conscious of!"

Letizia de Maigret, visual artist

"I love how easily I can connect the Flo that I know to what she has shared in her book. Her personality and character have underpinned her personal growth, but her expatriate experiences have added color, texture and importantly a self-belief and contentment that rings true. She brings it all together in an engaging, authentic and positive way, and her absolute commitment to embracing and making the most of the life she and Alex have chosen is inspiring and convincing for would-be expats and 'already expats' alike."

Sarah Blomfield, global marketing manager

"A very personal and transparent account of Flo's experience as an expat, which can help some wives who are facing a similar choice."

Marina Glendinning, full-time mother

"As I close this book, I am left with the beautiful feeling that we are so much more than we think we are! Through her journey, Florence shows us that when you allow yourself to dream and dare, life does not only give you back the gift of people but the one of discovering yourself. This book encourages everyone to cherish life and friendship to the fullest and always make the best of every opportunity."

**Caroline Rossi de Rosière,
expat and mother of three**

"This book is... a gift about Florence's experience based on real facts about how to turn something hard and difficult into something wonderful. It's all the author's authentic attitude with a touch of curiosity. Florence takes us on a trip around the world. After reading it, I wish I could fly all over the world. Thank you for your happiness Florence!"

**Monica Hernàndez, Mexican,
Ironman and mother of five**

"Flo is one of those people everybody likes and it's because of her attitude. Attitude is everything, and in this book, Flo will share her lessons learned and help you to have a positive, curious and 'can-do' attitude which will enrich your expat life. I would recommend this book to all future and current expats."

**Nanette Zwaan, development manager in
the arts and cultural sector**

"A very personal and honest story of an experienced expat wife showing you the ups and downs of living abroad and in different countries for many years. It really made me want to travel and immerse myself into different cultures again."

Author and founder and designer of Emilia Ohrtmann

"Florence paints the expat life in glorious color with her vast number of experiences and insights. For anyone curious about expat life, this book will not only show you the possibilities but also help you to reflect on whether it is the right choice for you."

Jane Saddler, life coach, teacher and mother of three

ACKNOWLEDGEMENTS

Nothing in my life path predestined me to write a book, especially in English, and yet when the idea was born, I was surrounded by such enthusiasm from the people I love, that writing this book has been a magical journey.

I must start with my husband Alexander Reisch. My rock, my husband, but above all my teammate who since we met listens to me and encourages me in everything I do. His constant positive energy and dynamism motivates me to take up the challenges that come my way. Alex is very present, trusts me and also supports me to promote my success. By living with Alex, there is never a dull moment. As he says, "life is rich but you need to go for it!" Thank you, Alex, for such a rich and intense life!

A big thank you to Mindy Gibbins-Klein, my publisher, who trusted me from the first time we met. It was a gamble for you too, as I came with just a life story but no writing experience. Thanks to your experience, your rigorousness and your encouragement I could only believe in the outcome of my book. Three months to write a book was your promise, I believed you and I did it! Thank you, Mindy, for this crazy journey.

And thank you, of course, to her great team at Panoma Press for their hard work.

Thank you, Caroline Rossi de Rosière, for always valuing my attitude towards my expat life. Thank you for once telling me that my experiences would be so beneficial to someone who wanted to live a life full of adventure. This sentence was probably the seed that gave birth to this book. Merci ma Caro.

Thank you to my friend Kyra Dupont Troubetzkoy. Thank you for sharing with me your trust from the beginning when I told you about this idea. Thank you for believing in me when I told you I would like to share my life experience and my passion for coaching in a book. Coming from you, journalist and writer, it gave me a wonderful energy that accompanied me throughout my project. Merci ma Kyra.

Thank you to Imogen Parker, a gifted young student, passionate about English literature, who helped me with the English and the syntax. Thank you, Imi!

Thanks to Jane Saddler, a great coach, who generously took her precious time to carefully proofread and correct my writing. Thank you, Jane!

Thank you, Christina de Bavier, for your story and good luck in Dubai! No doubt you will love it!

To my expatriate friends who agreed to be my beta readers and to give me their precious feedback that made all the difference with the final version of the book. Thanks to Marina Glendinning, Caroline Rossi de Rosière, Monica Hernàndez, Nanette Zwaan, Letizia de Maigret, Emilia Ohrtmann and Sara Blomfield for being so honest and helpful. Thank you for your unique enthusiasm when I told you about my project and thank you for encouraging me along the adventure.

A special thank you to my coaching clients who inspire me every day by sharing often very intimate themes. Thank you for your trust, your honesty and your loyalty. Thank you for allowing me to be a mediator in your transformation. This book is also the reflection of my experience with you and the desire to share what you are teaching me and what I have learned from you.

To my readers, who will contribute to the success and spread of this book. I hope that my words will have a positive impact on your life, that you will read passages that will make you smile, reflect and inspire you.

Thank you for taking the time to read my book and for recommending it to other people you know who might find it useful.

And I could not conclude these thanks without thanking my large expatriate family. All these encounters have inspired me for over 25 years. To all of those who have accompanied me on my journey, who have helped me grow and become the woman I am today.

Thank you also to Alex's employer with whom a mutual trust was created and who has enabled us to travel around the world and have an amazing life!

CONTENTS

INTRODUCTION

Over the past 25 years, I have been what you can call a serial expat around the world. After moving from one continent to another every three to five years for all those years, I am now settled here in Dubai for who knows how long?

I am now leaving a chapter behind to start a new one. I am in the process of a new transition: the end of my nomadic life for a more stable life.

It was while looking back on those beautiful years with a heavy heart and a lot of nostalgia, that I really felt the need to take action to accept this situation and help myself through this period in a positive way. Writing this book was my way of closing an important chapter of my life in a peaceful and free way, and welcoming the next one with freedom and motivation.

Reflecting on all these extraordinary years, I was also at a point in my life where I felt the need to share my gratitude and appreciation for all the people who have contributed to making my expatriate life an amazing and successful journey.

To my friends, I hope they will accept this book as a message of acknowledgement and thanks for all the great years we have shared.

To my family, I have always wished that my children would re-live our adventure: their parents' story and their own. Writing this book is also my way of leaving Constantin and Angelina a legacy. I wanted my children to remember the energy, the values and the spirit in which we evolved: a family united, present for each other and eager for new discoveries.

I felt the need to re-live all those moments and unique experiences that have fulfilled my family and myself.

To all future expatriates, current expatriates or anyone curious about expatriation, I felt the need to share my story because deep down I know I would have loved to read a book like this at some point in my expatriate life. A book that resonates with me, that reassures me about the life stages I am going through, those that await me and how I can anticipate them, to live them with positivity and confidence. I wanted to offer other women what I have received: an opportunity to create the life that was designed for me. My desire is to share any objective input that could help you make the right decision and be confident that everything will work out because the choice you made was one of self-confidence.

This has been a life where the world was offered to me, along with the opportunity to enjoy an extremely happy family life, discover new cultures, and meet wonderful people. A life during which I was also very involved in the many roles I took on. Though it has emotionally challenged me often, this life has made me determined, happy and passionate.

A life during which my encounters and my connections also played an essential role in my personal development; an aspect of my life that I wish to pursue with the writing of this book and my coaching career.

This book is therefore addressed to any person, wife, mother, partner or individual who has thought about a new career as an expatriate, who chooses this nomadic life or who is considering going abroad. It offers a practical and psychological approach to what expatriate life is like. I share many personal stories, learnings and anecdotes. I also invite the reader to self-reflect on various themes. I hope that my life experiences will inspire you to embrace or pursue this nomadic life.

As with every experience, my story is distinct and unique in itself. However, it is interesting to note that many of the situations I encountered along the way are ultimately common to all expatriates.

I am aware that not all expatriates go on expatriation under the same conditions. So, whether you are going with a private company, with an NGO or as a freelancer, most of the themes discussed will likely be equally relevant to your own experience. For this reason, and so that all types of expatriates can find information that resonates with them, I have chosen to write this book by theme and not chronologically.

In this book, I also wanted to share with you my passion for coaching and invite my readers to discover how this tool can have an extremely powerful impact on the personal development of each individual. I was inspired by coaching as a communication tool because it allows me to reach out and connect with other women who also want to progress, transform and grow to achieve their dreams by working on their skills, values and strengths.

At the end of each chapter, you will be invited to reflect on questions related to the chapter's theme. Each question is there to clarify your vision and create a new perspective as you have decided to make a change in your life. There is no right or wrong answer. Each answer depends on you, on your experience of the situation and on what you want for yourself and your loved ones. These questions are simply meant to guide you in your thinking.

My hope is that every reader will find a little inspiration in my book that will make them rethink their perspective about their current situation and their future.

Let it go! What won't happen if you don't do it? Think not only about the consequences of doing something or taking that risk, but also about the consequences of not taking the plunge.

Enjoy your reading!

CHAPTER

ONE

Being one with your partner is important

What an earthquake in my dream life when my boyfriend came home from work and told me that his company had offered him an expatriate position in Cotonou, Africa!

My first thought was, "where the hell is Cotonou?"

Let's put things in context...

I was 25 years old at the time, I had my degree in communications, I was a product manager in a highly-rated communications company, my social life was busy and fun, I had my own flat, I had freedom, and above all I was in love! Life was good for me, and I did not feel the need to change anything!

But...

I remember the sparkle in Alex's eyes when he told me about his dream promotion. Alex, originally from Austria, grew up as an ambassador's child in Kenya and always told me that he would like to return to Africa one day.

At that moment my heart made the decision for me. I declared that we would go to Africa together! It was certainly the most spontaneous and, looking back, also the best decision I have ever made in my life! Something I would realize only years later!

This was when our adventure started. Alex gave me the choice and I made my decision. It was a neutral situation; we had no obligation to each other.

The Excitement (with a capital E) started; Alex took out a ream of paper to show me all the research he had done in the last few hours on Cotonou (Benin) and the things to do there... still today, I am curious to leaf through those documents, as I am sure that only the first two pages were printed. Those who lived in Cotonou in the 2000's will agree that the activities were clearly limited! This was a discovery I would only make a few months later, once I had settled there.

Mine and Alex's relationship was still in the early stages. We had been together for just over a year but like most women who go abroad (if not for our own careers), I followed my heart, and went abroad out of love. Our relationship was very easy and natural. We were always together, we had lots of fun, we laughed a lot, we had great friends and the world was ours!

When I told my father about my plans to follow Alex to Africa, he immediately invited us home for dinner and naturally asked Alex what his "plans" were with his daughter.

With great assurance, Alex reassured my father that he had no plans, which meant no commitments, and that my father should not worry too much. "Miss Hermes" would certainly be back after three weeks; he did not expect me to stay for long...   That was 25 years ago, we are now married with two children, Constantin and Angelina. We have lived on five continents, Africa, Indonesia, Brazil, Mexico, Philippines and now we are living in Dubai. We have no intention of returning to either Switzerland or Austria!

The beginnings...

Alex's generosity has certainly been the key to my growth and ease of settlement in each new country. Alex always made me feel like his priority and went out of his way to meet my urgent needs. His loving and caring attitude encouraged me to be active, responsible and motivated to organize a happy life for myself during his work and for us when he got off work and at weekends.

However, the early days of expatriation can be challenging but the good news is that, with some initial effort, moving to another country can become a fun undertaking and a really fulfilling experience.

During the first weeks following my arrival in Cotonou, I was confronted with the feeling of isolation. I suddenly found myself alone from Monday to Friday from 8am to 12pm and from 3pm to 7pm. Fortunately, Alex was coming back for lunch.

At the time, I had a very limited internet connection, so there was very little opportunity to call my friends and family back home. In any event, I think this kind of communication would have helped me only to a certain extent as the context of our relationships was now different. My friends and family had their lives, their routines, and I had chosen a different life. I had to move on. You have to know that I am a person who thrives on contact and exchange. Connection is what energizes me the most!

In expatriation, this feeling of isolation is certainly the main difference between a working partner and a "trailing spouse" (expat jargon for an expat partner) – a horrible metaphor in my opinion, one that sounds very passive and does not fit my life at all. I really see myself alongside my husband and certainly not behind him. I hope that through this book, you as a partner, whether you are a man or a woman, will value the important role you play as an individual in the success of the expatriate couple. Expatriation as a couple is a partnership, a team spirit between two individuals, a complementarity that aims to weld a couple together and hopefully create a lasting relationship.

Coming back to my need to get in touch with other people, I mean that the possibilities of contact with other people at the beginning of a new expatriate life were obviously very different for Alex and for me. The work partner, Alex, is experiencing continuity: he has his job, a new setting, new responsibilities that require him to be very focused and he is already in a routine.

Alex was connected and intellectually busy all day. For him, going home was a chance to relax and certainly not to talk business. However, for me, conversation was a necessity to avoid sadness and depression. This is where the chemistry and the communication between you and your partner really becomes a must: listening, sensing, understanding and respecting each other's needs and feelings to improve your partner's life.

Share your feelings...

At the beginning, I had to make this point and I had to insist upon effective communication because Alex was not used to sharing so many details, but we got there. It was my way of ensuring a continuity with my past life! To stay in the flow of my life.

I was very honest with Alex, I needed to be 100% part of his life for my own sanity: I thought I needed to visualize his situations, imagine his feelings; it gave me a sense of life, of belonging. This effective and emotive communication gave me energy for the day: it motivated me, encouraged me to move forward, be creative and get out of my comfort zone.

Every day I encouraged Alex to share his work experiences, emotions and stories with me. In Africa, life is very joyful and there is a lot of laughter, so naturally I wanted him to tell me everything! I needed to be part of his experience; I did not want to be left alone on the side of the road. I was looking for a sense of inclusion, and I felt I had to be the person Alex could count on for this life adventure. I needed to find my role in this journey. My survival mindset was already active.

I can only reassure you that women are courageous and have unexpected strengths!

Successful communication...

To be honest, I remember crying a few times in Africa, wondering if I had made the right choice, if leaving everything behind had been wise, but my tears always dried up because I deeply loved what I was experiencing. The discovery of another world, I was in love with Love, and the adventure was stronger than what I had left behind.

From the very beginning of our expatriate adventure, I felt that the complicity and love between Alex and I was becoming increasingly intense, that we were putting all our passion for life into this adventure and that we were starting to build something strong. Six months later, we got engaged in South Africa and in November 2000 we got married on the island of Bom Bom off the coast of Gabon with a few close friends and our family. So now I am committed to following my soulmate to live the expat life!

If communication had been important to me back then, it has continued to be absolutely essential ever since. I believe that communication and continuous exchange are the key to a fulfilling long-term relationship and life in expatriation. If in the beginning it is to avoid isolation, later on it is to avoid a new trap: distanciation.

Let me explain: as time goes by, women find their way and are busy with activities, new appointments, often children and without noticing it, your partner suddenly finds themself outside of this new world you have naturally created. No one blames you for this, because in the end, this is what you have been asked to do to fit into your new life, but the reality is that your partner is not involved, unless you, in turn, encourage him/her to share your life!

Here's a tip: no matter how hectic your life is, make it a habit to have one night a week for romantic time: hire a babysitter, book a restaurant, play sports together, get together to do something you've always enjoyed doing as a couple. Developing your complicity is an essential ingredient for your success as an expat couple!

Define your role...

In my experience, defining the roles of each person in a relationship brings about freedom, responsibility and fulfilment. These are three elements which, if not present, can also be the main reasons for the failure of an expatriation.

Obviously, every individual experiences each situation in a different way, and I would like to take a moment to emphasize that I am only talking about what *I* have experienced: my own experience, my own feelings. I invite you to take from this book what resonates with you and leave the rest aside. My way is obviously not the only way. So, with this in mind, I will continue with my own unique experience.

As life progresses, I have found it important to define the roles of each person in the couple, especially in extraordinary situations or with regard to children, for example. In our case, after twenty years of expatriation, my husband was sent to Pakistan, a country where the company he works for did not recommend that the family move there. So, we had the choice of either "splitting up" and living in a split family situation, or giving up the promotion entirely.

Believe it or not, such a big decision in an expat's life has to be taken in 24 hours. Headquarters do not wait; business is business… that's the reality!

Having other families around me who had experienced so-called split family situations, myself and Alex had previously discussed the scenario. At the time it was clear that we could never accept this arrangement. In my mind, it was clear that an expatriation was a situation in which one lives as a united family; there was no question of separating. But the reality is quite different... The lesson I learned from this experience is that until you are in the situation yourself, you never really know how you will react. Eventually my decision was the opposite of the one I had imagined when the situation applied to another family.

Despite our preconceived ideas, at this moment, your mind goes very fast and you consider the benefits, the risks and the consequences for yourself and for your family.

Suddenly you make the connection between your unique life experience, your current state of mind, your emotions and your own perspective on the situation. Understanding and identifying the impact of all these elements on your own life will enable you to make your own decision, the one that fits who you are as an individual in this particular situation.

This is how other people's experiences become their story and are no longer directly related to ours.

At the time of the event, Alex was in Switzerland, 11,000km away from home in Manila, when the head office offered him this promotion in Pakistan. All our discussions were done by phone. Out of respect for me, knowing that I was against the separation of the family, Alex had already refused the job... I was speechless!

I could not withhold my curiosity so I had to ask him what his perspective was on this promotion. Alex spontaneously replied that it was a professional challenge he would have loved to take up, a way to end his career in apotheosis.

So, it was clear, the final decision was in my hands. Was I ready to make this compromise for the sake of my husband? For the record, I immediately called my dad, who only gives advice when asked. His answer was clear. "You can't stop a man from excelling in his career." My dad's message hit home and it was obvious to me that I would do anything to support my husband in his career.

Knowing Alex, his sensitivity, his commitment to the family and his empathy, I knew that if I accepted the split living arrangement, Alex would be so driven by this new challenge, that he would do everything possible to make his family happy in our new life. We would find a solution so that each of us would maintain our balance and not suffer from this physical separation. Alex would make the effort to come home every weekend and he would devote himself to his family. I would be supported in my choices about our children and my life. I would never feel judged by him, but rather, respected.

The decision was finally made very genuinely. It was a real gesture of love and respect. I really wanted to give him his freedom to embrace the opportunity and grow through the gratification of his work and his career.

I was conscious that this decision would be a major compromise for me, but this new life challenge came at a time when Alex and I had already resolved many situations in positive ways. Our past experiences had shown me that I could also trust the process. I was confident that as a team we could do it!

It was once again an opportunity for renewal: we each had a new challenge ahead of us. But like every start, this new adventure inspired us, motivated us, energized us and made us stronger. I also wanted to believe that on Alex's part, it was a way of valuing my commitment as a mother, leaving me with responsibility for our children.

When the roles reversed ...

After three and a half years in Africa, we were transferred to Jakarta, Indonesia. Alex's start with his new boss unfortunately did not go at all as planned. Alex came back every night more and more discouraged and even wanted to resign from the multinational company that had inspired him so much until now. It was like an electric shock for me: my rock, my always-so-positive man, was shrinking in front of me; I could not recognize him anymore.

I remember when it occurred to me that I had two choices: to fade away with him or to take the reins, to continue fighting and pursue our dream, living this expat life that we already loved so much.

All my focus went on him. I had to think and react quickly. Alone, I knew I wouldn't be strong enough, I needed people Alex trusted, role models who had inspired him and who had gone through the same ordeals and who would give him a good kick in the butt...

I called Alex's father and two of his very close friends that I knew would be there for him. The coincidence was that Alex had to fly back to Switzerland for a seminar. Perfect timing for his friends and family to meet him and give him the support he needed during this tough transition.

Meanwhile, in Jakarta, I had started to settle following our move and was able to welcome Alex back from Switzerland to a new, cozy, loving, well-organized and settled home: his past few months were just a bad memory; his friends, his father and I did what was necessary to make him start with a new perspective. The dynamic had changed, we were starting afresh.

The irony of this story is that I got pregnant naturally after four years of unsuccessful fertility treatment.

There must be some truth to this advice for women who are bent on getting pregnant: it seems that one of the quickest ways to help stop obsessing about your own difficulties is to do something for someone else. Volunteer at a worthy organization, participate in a fundraiser, do several random acts of kindness, become a mentor, reach out to a friend in need. Well, this advice definitely worked for me.

At this stage, it's also important to mention that studies show that the two main reasons for early expat assignment termination are if the husband/working partner has difficulty adjusting to his new professional situation and if the wife/partner does not integrate into her new environment. And yes, it is important to remember that sometimes you even have the opposite scenario, where the wife is very happy and the husband is struggling to adapt to his new situation, even though it was his job that brought them into this new life....

Through my story, I would like to emphasize how important your role as wife and, later for me, as a mother is in the expat family. Ladies, remember, you are playing a major role in the success of an expatriate life!

Self-esteem plays an important role in expat life...

All emotions experienced outside by your children and your spouse will be brought back to your home. Being the pillar of the house, you will be the receiver of all the feelings they have outside. Home will be your family's comfort zone, their only familiar place. It is at home that all their emotions will come out. Home is where an individual feels love, trust, support, encouragement and is what makes your family united.

Therefore, realizing our real role and responsibilities which, trust me, will be put to the test from the very beginning of any expatriation, can encourage us to adopt the right mindset from the start. Developing your self-esteem at this point can be a life changer.

Self-esteem in this context would mean: feeling aligned with your values and your choices, accepting yourself as you are, identifying your needs and addressing them. To keep a positive mindset and be a problem solver.

The real commitment of each party in expatriation...

It is interesting to observe that when one goes on expatriation, one expects the accompanying partner to naturally take on the different roles that allow the couple and the family to settle down, adapt and live this new experience to the fullest. Roles that are, in the end, a real job, that require a lot of positive energy, time and personal qualities. A job that is essential but not directly remunerated.

If at the beginning, we live these roles as privileges and as a gift, I would like to share here an observation that could be useful to our future or young expatriates to anticipate the expatriate life in the long term.

The years go by and there comes a phase in the life of the expatriate partner where he can organically ask himself the question of how he will be able to reintegrate into professional life after all these years of disconnection. Whether it is following the termination of an expatriation contract, a separation, a grief, the approach of the departure of the children from home or another change of life, I have seen how this question is natural but provokes a certain anxiety and fear in the life of the accompanying person.

I would therefore like to think that the partner, by leaving his stable situation, has in fact another duty and this one is a duty towards himself: that of thinking about himself, his personal development, his ambitions, in order to anticipate his own future and be able to return to active life if he so wishes.

It is in fact an extension of his professional career or his life as a student. The partner does not have to give up his dreams when he leaves his country, but he has to adapt them to his new life, to the means offered to him by his host country. Of course, this requires an extra effort, but I must admit that I feel the need to share this because around me, I see how not having thought about it can be a very strong and destabilizing element in the life of some partners. As I get older, I meet a lot of women who, for various reasons, are faced with this dilemma. They ask themselves what they will do once the current situation changes.

With the benefit of hindsight, I think this is an extremely important subject to discuss with your partner from the very beginning of the expatriation experience. Agreeing on the investment that this expatriation represents for both parties, so that each one finds his compensation, always feels equal and fair.

Discussing important matters...

Quitting your job means also leaving your financial independence. From my experience, and conflicts I have seen around me in expatriation, this is a delicate but essential subject that needs to be discussed before moving.

How is it going to happen? Everyone has a different relationship with money. Everyone manages and spends money in their own way, and it is not an exaggeration to say that the subject of money can quickly become the essence of war.

Personally, I had never talked about it at the beginning of our life in Africa. As we didn't have a bank account, I had to systematically ask for cash to buy groceries for the house or for my own personal purchases. Although Alex never made any remarks, it took me many years to feel comfortable. Today, the situation has changed. On the one hand I feel part of my husband's success and on the other hand, most of the expenses are for the family and for the children, so they are useful, necessary or discussed as a couple. But still, when it comes to me, I always have a little voice holding me back... I spend with an eye on what Alex would find acceptable.

Also, each country has its own rules regarding work visas for spouses, so make sure you know the conditions of your host country and then decide if the answer gives you access to the lifestyle you want.

Reflections...

To help identify your feelings about the expatriation life, I invite you to reflect on these questions:

- What makes you curious about expatriate life?

- What makes the expatriation move a difficult decision for you?

- How would you like to feel and think at the end of this book?

CHAPTER

TWO

Leaving one's country to live elsewhere is a unique experience that provokes many emotions

Taking each of my expat experiences independently, the first thing that comes to my mind is that I have always gone through different phases in each new place: the first phase was the honeymoon period, everything is new, everything is sublime. The second phase is the crisis phase, the reality phase: culture shock. You have to change your habits and adapt to the culture of the host country. The third phase is that of adjustment, you have developed understanding and you are in harmony with the country. The last phase: adaptation, you no longer want to leave the country to which you are now attached.

During each of these phases there are naturally ups and downs, I have experienced them too and I think you have to accept that this is quite normal. I remember the "honeymoon" period as a time of great excitement but at that time I was still a bit of a tourist and not yet local. That said, finding this excitement every time I move confirms in my heart that I am really made for this kind of life. A life of constant adaptation.

On the other hand, it always took me six months, almost to the day, from the moment I landed in the country to when I sat down on my sofa and said to myself: this is *my* home: home sweet home. This feeling also marks the real beginning of my life there: when I start to get my bearings, my habits and I see my family blossom.

In two different countries, we had to spend six months in a hotel before moving into our own house. For me, these transition periods are the most difficult but, as I was mentioning, also very exciting ones. I know that for many expatriates these are periods that are even described as "psychological torture." They are often long periods of waiting, of doubts and uncertainties, which delay our adaptation in the country.

Personally, I think it is great to be able to travel around the world with our own furniture. Our house really tells the story of our life. Every object has its own story. To immerse ourselves in a new country, we have always needed, as a family, to be surrounded by our belongings; it is our way of feeling at home in our new country. Something I could really observe with both our kids is the importance of organizing their room for themselves.

Usually, an expatriate assignment lasts between three and five years. Among expatriates, we also caricature our expatriations by saying that the first year is the year of adaptation, the second the year of adjustment and the third the year of transition.

This is because some companies, by internal policy or by agreement with the host country, impose "local employee status" after a certain number of years in the same country. This puts an end to an expatriate contract and often to the advantages that are related to it. This explains why expatriate assignments are often limited in time.

Usually, when two expats meet for the first time, within the first conversation you will have those few questions:

"Where are you from?"

"How long have you been here for?"

"How do you like it here?"

"Do you know where you are going next?"

Settling in...

I could compare my arrival in each country as turbulent landings, experienced each time in a different way. This is because we live different phases of our lives and because each previous experience fortunately softens the abrupt landing in the next country.

If I think about my arrival in Africa, besides the initial isolation and the total mystery of my life as part of a couple in a faraway country, it was finding myself that was important. I had to face the question: who are you when you are by yourself?

When I think about the second posting, Jakarta, the biggest challenge for me was the language as well as living in the largest Muslim country in the world where women in the Indonesian Muslim culture have a different status. Whilst in Africa I was part of many of Alex's professional trips and social events, but in Indonesia things changed. By the culture of the country, men gathered without women and the rules of the company had also started to change – I was no longer invited to travel with my husband when he was away.

The third posting was Curitiba in Brazil. I arrived with a baby, not speaking a word of Portuguese, in an industrial city, far from the dream expatriation that one may imagine when thinking of the beaches of Copacabana. The climate of Curitiba was also a challenge for me – when I think about it now, I feel as if I have been cold for three years.

The fourth posting was Mexico, with a second child. I had Portuguese in my pocket but I had to learn Spanish, an additional language. I also had to accept that living in the center of Mexico City, my dream, was not going to be an option.

The fifth posting was Manila, in the Philippines. After five years of bliss, we left Mexico, heartbroken, to discover the Philippines, a country impressive for the resilience of its people, who move from one natural disaster to another. By this time the children had also grown up and their adaptation to a new curriculum in a new language presented me with a new challenge which I obviously took very much to heart.

Last but not least, our sixth posting was in Dubai: having the split family experience, complete with all the emotions that this experience generates.

Each expatriate family goes through a unique journey. The destinations are different, but my experiences have shown me that the emotions are mostly similar.

However, in retrospect, I like to look back and think of all the memories. I feel really fulfilled and proud of my life experiences. That's what I think is most enlightening: I really feel like I'm living the life I was meant to live!

I believe that each of us individuals, expat or non-expat, is responsible for the life we live. We choose to be either the victims or actors of our lives. Even though I admit to having a very privileged life, I think I could have lived a totally different life if I had not chosen to take control of it and been bold enough to leave what I had, to live a very different kind of life. The material factors, although they obviously help, do not make all the difference. For me, attitude is a key factor.

The importance of your attitude...

Moni's motto... "*actitud es todo!*" (which means in Spanish: "attitude is everything"). With her deep voice, Moni, my Mexican "*hermana del alma*," a beautiful Mexican term to say "soul sisters," always used these words when it was time to join forces. I really feel the power of these words, they are always in my mind. Attitude is actually a state of mind!

If you are going on your first expatriate experience without knowing your strengths, do not worry – you will discover them along the way. Every life experience will be like a mirror for you. You will be continually surprised and impressed by what you achieve. Trust your instincts, try new things – the sky's the limit!

While living in Africa, I experienced a sense of peace and comfort in painting. This discovery was made without much expectation when, 25 years ago, I joined Henri's painting class. Henri was a French painter, also an expatriate, as he had followed his wife who had a teaching position at the French Lycée in Cotonou. Henri had a very poetic side, he was really passionate about drawing and painting. You could see that he had already adapted well to the African rhythm. He was always sharing with us how happy he was in Africa; he hoped to develop a business and stay there forever.

Henri had the reputation of being very good at simply teaching the necessary techniques that would lead his students to paint beautiful canvases. He knew how to pass on his passion and techniques to his students. I discovered oil painting with him and I remember doing some beautiful paintings of African life. I loved my classes and painted a lot on my own at home.

Unfortunately, I only had the chance to attend his classes for a short year because his wife's contract was not renewed and he had to return to France. Like many expatriates in this situation, this abrupt and unchosen break was the cause of a difficult return to France for him. A few years later, I was happy to learn that he had found a role that allowed him to share his passion again.

Henri will always remain in my heart because thanks to this uncomplicated introduction to painting, I also discovered a form of creativity in myself that I did not know I had. This manual experience made me want to try many other activities and I found myself making fabric boxes, porcelain painting and designing jewelry. Since then, painting has become my therapy. Like others would do yoga, I paint when I am stressed or nervous. While writing this book, I realized that I also like to paint during periods of transition, between moves when I think too much. It's a way for me to relax and stop overthinking.

While it is true that in this book I am talking particularly about expatriate women, as this is my experience, I would like to mention that more and more men today are also choosing this role. I have often met men who have chosen to follow their wives who have obtained the expatriation contract. I have also met couples who have decided from the start of their experiences that at the end of each contract, the roles would be reversed. In turn, the wife would follow her husband, then at the end of the contract, the man would follow the wife. These are other life experiences which I obviously cannot talk about as I have not experienced them myself but these scenarios are becoming more and more common.

Surprise, surprise...

Living abroad means accepting the consequence that you will live day to day, not knowing what tomorrow brings. Not knowing what comes next. If you ask Alex, he will tell you these are exactly the exciting reasons why he wanted to leave Switzerland. If some companies offer limited duration contracts, with an eventual return to the country of origin, in our case, we are supposed to stay between three and five years in a foreign country, without returning to Switzerland between posts.

Therefore, our daily life can be interrupted at any time. The routine we have set up for ourselves, the efforts we have made to integrate into the culture of a country can suddenly be disrupted, and we have to switch our attention to the next destination with the wave of a magic wand. The average time from the moment of the announcement to the day you are dropped in your new country is usually three months.

The difficulty and our duty at that moment is not to rush the departure. Out of respect for the country and for our friends, a nice farewell party is an opportunity to thank all those who have made this place our home, the place where we felt comfortable. I remember how challenging it was for me to keep this attitude as my feelings were already overwhelmed. My instinctive behavior has always been that as soon as Alex came home with the announcement of a new move, my mind was already projecting itself onto the next stage. I was already thinking about what to organize for the next transition.

For us, new things have always meant excitement and we have always wanted to continue discovering new countries. For some people (and I totally respect their decision) at a certain point expatriation no longer meets their needs and values. They would like to offer something else to their loved ones. This is a phenomenon that often occurs when children reach a certain age or when grandparents start to age and we feel too far from our family. The expatriate begins to feel the need to return to his or her roots and culture.

For us, moving to the next assignment was often moving to a new continent! For the record, Alex always mentioned in his preferences that he would like to stay 10 degrees north or south of the equator line. The good news is that we have always lived in a pleasant climate! Alex is also known professionally for his ability to turn around businesses in emerging countries, so we never ended up in New York, Paris or London!

What does it mean to be in transition...

In terms of emotions, transition means leaving your home for a new house, in an unfamiliar place, without landmarks or habits. It means leaving behind the friends who shared your daily life. It's managing the transition for you and your family from the moment the move is announced to the moment everyone feels comfortable in their new life. It's about being a role model for your children and ensuring that they feel confident in their new environment. It's about managing stress, excitement, anxiety, enthusiasm, curiosity, sadness, uncertainty, confidence, doubt, assurance and loneliness.

When you arrive in a new country, you can also go through a period of doubting yourself. In Africa, this was the case for me. When I first moved, I was not taking a big risk trusting my instincts because I did not have anyone else to worry about. But six years later I had my first child, Constantin and then Angelina three years later. My responsibilities had changed, I was not alone anymore, so I had to consider the consequences of my decisions more carefully.

I would ask myself more questions: what would this new country offer my family, and for how long? How would each of us live this experience? Today, I know that these questions are well-founded, as both my children have clearly experienced their new environments in different ways. Maybe because my life is unpredictable, I always liked to have a vision, some ambitions for my family and my children. Thinking one, three or five years ahead has always given me a red line to follow, a way to give myself a sense of direction, of security.

The feeling of guilt is also very strong when you have to tell your children about such a change. Each time, I knew that I was going to uproot them, take away their bearings, take them away from their comfort zone, their peacefulness and their friends – the life that they had built with resilience.

Each individual – and here I would like to speak specifically about expatriate children – experiences change and separation differently. While expatriation opens up new horizons and forges their personality with an ability to embrace change and open up to other cultures, for many children it is also a life that prevents them from being grounded, from forging deep friendships. Some protect themselves from investing fully in the friendship because they know that one day they or others will leave. Of course, social media helps to keep in touch, but it is heartbreaking every time it happens and some children are really scarred by the experience.

Although it is true that at the age of 10, 12 or later, in adolescence, this situation is particularly difficult to live with, I think that from a very young age, the child remembers this painful emotion of separation and handles it differently according to his personality. Personally, I experienced it with my son Constantin who, since the Philippines, has always preferred to anticipate this situation and protect himself. My daughter Angelina, on the other hand, has always lived her friendships to the fullest and suffered a lot afterwards.

Leaving beautiful friendships behind you...

Another of life's little gifts: at the very beginning of my time in Mexico, I can remember Constantin's first tennis lesson. It was one of my first outings, and I was in search of new activities and also new encounters. A very beautiful tall Mexican woman was sitting next to me. With my few words of Spanish, I introduced myself; very kindly, and seeing that I had already used up all of my Spanish vocabulary, Gaby immediately spoke to me in English. She had been studying in Switzerland for a year and the more we talked about our lives, the more we discovered that we had friends in common.

Of course, this coincidence created an immediate bond. However, Gaby, despite being an extremely kind, gentle and sensitive woman, very quickly shared with me how frustrating she found friendships with expatriate women. She had obviously already suffered a very hard time losing valuable relationships with expatriate women who had subsequently left Mexico. It is interesting to note here that it is not always the one who leaves the country who suffers the most.

From what she said, I assumed that Gaby would not push for a close friendship as the discussion was not going in a very optimistic direction, but life had a different plan for us.

This meeting took place 13 years ago, and fast forward to today, this friendship has been one of the most beautiful things that Mexico has offered me.

Like other mothers in Mexico, Gaby and Moni have this vocation to offer their time and open their hearts to share with society their religious faith, which in Mexico is an extremely strong value. So, I was fortunate that my son was prepared for his first communion by two friends dear to my heart. For me, this episode has only enriched our friendship. Gaby and I had boys of the same age; Jose-Pablo and Constantin were in the same class at school and together in all the after-school activities. They became very close friends. Even today we still meet up during the holidays; they are families who travel a lot and we always manage to meet somewhere in the world.

During our stay in Mexico, Gaby and I created many memories that today keep us connected. I do not think there is a month that goes by without us talking or exchanging messages. Gaby and her family mean a lot to all of us.

In expatriation, we often talk about culture shock. The word expatriate comes from the Latin terms, *ex* "out of" and *patria* "native country, homeland." This term explains perfectly the concept of leaving our country, our culture, to go and meet another culture.

If I take the example in Mexico, the religion being common to ours, the children lived with our religious values without having to adapt. In other countries, such as Indonesia or here in Dubai, all four of us had to learn to adapt and respect the local religion.

This example of intercultural adjustment requires a readaptation to cultural differences. Sometimes we have to give up or change our usual ways of living and thinking. This intercultural adjustment is also part of the expatriate's efforts. Adapting to cultural differences is also a sign of respect towards our host country and facilitates integration. I am talking about religion here, but another example of integration is obviously learning the language of the country. This is also an essential factor for better enculturation.

What inspires me...

What continues to give me confidence in my family's choice of life, stronger than all the negative emotions that can go through my head and my heart, is undoubtedly the bond that we have developed between the four of us as well as the bond that the children have between them. The trust, knowing that we are really present for each other, the natural communication that has taken place, the moments of happiness that we share, the important time that we spend together, the memories that we build, so many moments of laughter, joy, complicity. For all these invaluable reasons, I know I am where I want to be!

Maybe now that I talk about my family's emotions you are wondering how I simultaneously deal with my own emotions to get my life back in balance? As I mentioned before, the strength of the mother and the wife is essential, but for that, she must be well with herself, that is to say, have found her own balance.

Even if I have always experienced the transition period from one posting to another with enthusiasm, rejoicing to live a new adventure, I admit that those times of doubts, concessions and frustration that I talked about earlier always put me in a very sensitive state during these periods.

Looking for happiness and balance in the next place...

It all starts with the exploration trip: except for Africa, we always took the time to visit the country we were going to move to. This trip is always very emotional because it takes place over a short week and the objective is to discover the country from a half-tourist, half-professional angle. At this stage, you are already clearly committed to the company. Even if it is your last chance to decline the offer, you already feel very committed to the process. So even though I am extremely grateful to have been able to do these recon trips, I must admit that I have always been a bit tense during these days.

I will always remember my arrival in Curitiba, Brazil. Curitiba is an industrial city south of Sao Paulo. The airport was small. Batista, the driver, was waiting for us with a charming smile at the exit. The weather was very chilly, the sky was grey – a light rain, far from the tropical image I had of Brazil. We drove for miles on a straight road, there was nothing to see except some favelas at the entrance of the city. Alex and I spent the next 45 minutes driving without speaking to each other, our eyes staring at this landscape, probably looking for the trigger that would break the ice. Despite the fact that we were together, this was a moment of loneliness for me.

When we arrived at the hotel, Alex, certainly feeling our mood and always wanting to lighten the situation, decided with a lot of optimism to go and find a nice terrace in the city center. Off we went, to discover the city and its gems. However, with limited success, as the city did not look at all as we expected. We came back to the hotel and headed downstairs; our lunch came down to a *Bacalhau* in the formal dining room on the first floor of our hotel.

After visiting many houses, a few days later, we found a cute little house an equal distance between the school and Alex's office, the perfect isosceles triangle! Alex would even be able to drop our son on the way to the office. I started to feel the city and picture myself around it. The school was lovely, and I felt that my son would be happy there. Batista was such a nice person; he was also a good ambassador to his city. Even though I did not speak a word of Portuguese, the enthusiasm started to take over, the people all seemed very nice and welcoming.

I felt very quickly that Curitiba would offer us a better quality of life now that we were a small family and that our weekends would be different from those of a life without children. I could really imagine being happy and fulfilled there: the city was quiet, very green, lots of parks and places to walk with my son and my dog. I soon felt that I could easily move around and find my way around the city. After Jakarta, the idea of not being stuck in traffic and driving by myself was a relief. I did not feel that the culture shock would be too difficult, I just had to learn the language, which I was excited about. We were also reassured that Curitiba was one of the safest cities in Brazil in terms of security. Alex was already making me dream of all the trips he was planning, to discover Brazil and its neighboring countries.

Even though during this trip I could not meet other expats because Alex's arrival in Curitiba was not yet public, I already had a good feeling. I left Curitiba with a totally different perspective than when I arrived. I was now looking forward to this next adventure. I had reconnected with myself, I visualized myself in every place I had visited in Curitiba, this trip had given me confidence and I knew that this experience would be right for us at this time in our lives. I felt proud of my husband's promotion and I was ready to live it fully.

Leaving one's country to live elsewhere is a unique experience that provokes many emotions. However, it is essential to bear in mind that once the transition period is over, the experience will necessarily be personally enriching. If I think back on all my expatriations, it is obvious that I have some that I liked more than others, but they were all very rich and fulfilling in their own way.

Reflections...

To help identify your emotions about the expatriation life, I invite you to reflect on these questions:

- What emotions or behaviors tend to arise when you face changes in your life?

- What impact do these emotions or behaviors have on you as a person? (positive/ negative – how do you react/deal with them?)

- What resources do you have available to you?

CHAPTER

THREE

It is important to leave with the right company

The expatriate life attracts you, and you have chosen to commit to a certain company because you know that it offers opportunities to work abroad. However, before you take the plunge and begin this wonderful adventure, you must be curious about the steps involved in expatriation.

You express your interest...

You are interested in an expatriate position, so you apply or the company comes to you and offers you a position. The timing is often the first surprise: the announcement of this transfer often comes at a time when you are not expecting it. Be prepared, because, as I mentioned before, if you choose this nomad life, from then on you will probably be called upon to move regularly with little prior notice!

The briefing...

You are briefly told about the job and its responsibilities, given some information about the destination so that you can visualize what is on offer, and asked if you are interested. Your instincts will certainly help you make an initial decision and you should remember that rejections reduce the chances of being offered new opportunities.

The exploratory trip...

This is a way for you and the company to confirm your respective commitments. It is a first approach that will allow you to get an idea of the host country and to find out if an immersion on both a professional and personal level is possible for you. This exploratory trip is as important for the potential expat and their family as it is for the employer. A failed expatriation can have an extremely devastating impact on the employee and his/her family, as well as extremely high costs for the employer.

The package...

The package is a negotiation. Both parties have to be happy with what they give and what they get. This is what I would like to focus on as I have noticed that other expat families, who have poorly negotiated their package, have experienced anger or frustration.

Expatriations come and go, but they are never the same because families grow and need change over time: single life, getting married, having children and wanting to return home is normal. Knowing that a company follows the natural evolution of life gives a real feeling of confidence and knowing that the company will always support us and evolve with us in terms of remuneration and flexibility is very reassuring!

If the costs of an expatriation are important for the company, it is also all the administration that a transfer entails that is tedious. This is a very complicated part when you arrive in a country where you are not familiar with the system and there is a significant language barrier.

In most countries, before you can have access to a bank account, a telephone subscription or even the ability to rent a house, you need a residence visa. To get a residence visa, you need a work contract, a process that, without the support of an established company in the country, can take weeks and a lot of energy – precious energy that you need for everything else.

The relocation agency...

The company usually uses relocation agencies, which by definition help newcomers settle into their new country. In my family's case, the relocation agency handled all of the necessary administration, support to find a house and they organized appointments at the schools I chose to visit.

Even if the agency does its best to meet the criteria you put forward on a basic pre-filled questionnaire, it is difficult for them to know exactly what you are looking for. The person who takes care of you is also your first link with the new country. All your hopes are in them: what they will show you in the next few days will be the outline of your next life in this new city. As you visit, the relocation agent almost becomes your "best" friend. You have shared all your emotions with them, they may have seen you crying in despair or in euphoria, having words with your husband, and they obviously witnessed all the emotional ups and downs in this process. Honestly, as much as these few days testing out your new country are exciting, I also remember these visits as extremely emotional and draining.

Your relocation agent has recommended their best restaurants, favorite sights, the best shopping areas and maybe even a hair salon... you may even have developed a close relationship – but at the end of the exploration trip, will they have found you the house of your dreams in the perfect neighborhood? Will they have found the perfect school for your children?

This may not always be the case and I would recommend being prepared for this not to be the case and be ready to continue your search afterwards. Of course, the success of this trip all depends on the real estate market in the city as well as the time of year you are going to make your exploration trip, but the search for a home can be unpredictable. There is no rule; finding a house is very much a matter of luck. Also, it is true that in one week, it is often difficult to settle all the administrative arrangements, negotiate the rent and the dates of entry with the landlord. In short, one rarely has the contract of the house when leaving the trip.

Preparing for our trip, researching the country, being part of expat support groups on social networks: being proactive is what worked best for us! If we had not arrived in every country with antennas deployed and a lot of foresight, our lives would not have worked out as they did. They may well have been just as happy, but undoubtedly, they would have been very different. Discovering a country as a future citizen rather than a tourist is a very different approach, and you should take this into account.

In my experience, while it is essential to have a company or local help to support you in your first steps, personal commitment is essential to immerse yourself in the country from the start.

I sense this period of transition to be an emotional, sensitive and crucial part in my expatriation. In fact, I often felt like becoming a relocation agent myself. I felt that by being an expat myself, I would have greater closeness and connection with a newcomer, than a native who may never have moved in their life, and, therefore, did not quite understand the emotional aspect of the situation and could not put themselves in their clients' shoes.

Of course, the agent will have better detailed knowledge of his or her city and country than me, but will he or she have the contacts, the addresses that allow new expatriates to immerse themselves in their new world as quickly as possible? By being like the newcomer, a citizen of the world, a citizen of passage in this same city, I will probably be more informed on the trendy places, the latest shops, the shows to see, on the kind of very updated addresses that are constantly circulating in expat groups in the form of emails and groups on social media.

Even if it is not necessary to leave a first visit with all these details, it is true that having addresses that seem familiar and looking forward to the relocation, gives a lot of confidence in a new move. On the other hand, settling in a country and knowing from the beginning where to buy what you like, who to contact in case of emergency, having the coordinates of doctors who speak a common language, is really what makes the difference! It's only when you start to get used to your new life that everyone will make their own choices and finally live a unique experience in the same city.

The opportunity of working for a relocation agency came up in Mexico. The agency was in Polanco, a district in the center of Mexico City. I lived in Los Encinos, 35km away and the journey there would normally take 40 minutes by car except on the day of my job interview. I arrived three hours late. The traffic in Mexico City is terrible, you never know what time you will arrive at your destination. That morning, I saw my dream job turn into a nightmare. I realized that this job would have me spending long days sitting in my car, which was diametrically opposed to my aspiration to share my good addresses, my experiences and the joys of expat life in Mexico. At that moment, I preferred to give up this professional project and, later in my life, the opportunity to become a relocation agent did not present itself. Life evolved and other opportunities came up.

In the same spirit of supporting newcomers, while living in the Philippines, Alex's office HRD (human resources director) had the wonderful initiative of asking the spouses of their expatriate employees to welcome (without obligation) new families. A WhatsApp group brought together anyone who wanted to participate, and every month we would meet for a welcome lunch at each other's homes to meet fellow wives and share any tips we had. I think it was a brilliant and nice idea on the part of the HRD to empathize with their new colleagues and partners. This was a great way for them to mingle with their new colleagues. And let me tell you, no matter how many times you move, when you arrive as a stranger in a foreign land, those first lunches are marked with a red pen in your agenda, you will not miss them!

I also would like to take a moment to mention that in general, expats are extremely supportive of each other, especially in countries where life is more difficult. Wherever you go, you will find support and empathy, trust me!

Medical cover...

Depending on the country you are going to, negotiating good medical coverage is also an important point to discuss before you leave for your new country.

After four and a half years in Africa, we visited the Swiss Tropical Institute. A routine check-up for some people, but a lifesaver for my husband and I! A few days after our blood tests, the Swiss professor called my husband back urgently. Alex had a list of parasites as long as his arm: caught from the food, the drinking water and also the lagoons, the savannahs and the dream ecosystems in which we spent our weekends.

As for me, I was not spared and received a draconian treatment which completely cleaned my body. To this day, I still wonder if all these infections were the cause of my infertility for the last four years. But what a relief to think that despite all the fertility treatments I had done in Africa, nature had been stronger than I was and that I had not become pregnant at that time! Only a few months after completing this treatment when we had just arrived in Jakarta, I became pregnant. For their own reasons, the company preferred that I give birth in Singapore, rather than in Jakarta. This decision also resulted in significant additional costs, which were, in our case, thankfully covered by Alex's employer and our insurance.

Integration...

We always needed support to integrate new routines into our daily lives. For me, it was always important to learn the language of the country and I liked to enroll in language courses at university (a language diploma on a CV is always a plus). For both children and spouses, the company may give an allowance for language courses and personal development but this may vary from company to company. In our situation, the children have always been educated in a different language from home, so they have always needed support in lessons to develop their grammar and vocabulary. The cost of this has always been significant, but worth it.

As I mentioned earlier, I think it is important to discuss the financial investment and support that can be considered for the accompanying partner.

I won't go into detail about salaries, tax exemptions, overseas allowance and bonuses as all of these are specific to and dependent on the company, the position of the employee and the years spent in the company. Each company decides on its housing package and what this includes. In some cases, water, electricity and gas bills are paid and private telephone calls, TV and internet subscriptions are paid for by the expatriate.

Each company allocates an allowance to cover accommodation or a type of property. Negotiating the terms of payment and maintenance of the accommodation with the landlord is also an issue, and the help of an agency or employer can be very beneficial. In some cases, the company provides an allowance to furnish the house with the basic contents, or one has the chance to travel the world with one's furniture. In my case, travelling with my furniture has been an important element of my successful nomadic life. I was constantly able to travel with my story, my life, my adventures.

One may also be provided with a car and driver. In some countries, for security reasons, it is strongly discouraged or even forbidden to drive yourself. One or two return flights per year, or a change of scenery, are also offered to employees to spend time with their family at home or in a destination of their choice. For those who have children, their school fees are mostly covered.

In 25 years with our company, I have seen this package change from job to job and many of our benefits have disappeared or been replaced by other benefits. I have simply observed in my years of expatriation that only those expatriates who joined for the right reasons are still part of the adventure. If at the beginning one is attracted by the financial advantages of expatriation, very quickly the emotions that they may have been unprepared for catch up with them and this can be overwhelming.

On the other hand, the feeling of weariness can also appear with the years particularly when the moves become too frequent. It can be tiring to always have to recompose the same pattern of adaptation. Around me, many people, for different reasons, have tired of this nomadic life and decided to live closer to their family, friends and culture.

In short, the more prepared you are for your departure, the less you will clutter your mind with doubts and questions.

This free space leaves room for opportunities and all the nice surprises that expatriation can offer. If you are clear on the formalities and conditions of your expatriation, you now have the mind and heart to live this wonderful adventure!

To conclude this chapter, a metaphor comes to mind: if each expatriation was like a parachute jump, you should know everything about each step you will take leading up to the edge before taking the plunge. While you will have the company as your parachute, your security, you will still need to make sure you play your part in this move and adjustment.

Carpe diem! Live the moment, enjoy the surprise with an open mind!

Reflections...

To help identify your needs during the expatriate life, I invite you to reflect on these questions:

- What are your non-negotiable needs?

- What are you ready to give up?

- What benefits would have to be offered for you to accept the conditions of expatriation?

CHAPTER

FOUR

Reflection will be the key that will help you make the right decisions for you and your family

Now that you are reassured about the company and the process of moving, I think it is important to refocus on yourself and your loved ones in order to analyze the direct impact that moving abroad will have on you and on your family members.

I would like to remind you that it is both our right and duty to make our own decisions; just as we respect the decisions of others, our decisions must be respected.

In the case of an expatriation as a couple or family, I believe it is important that the accompanying partner is an integral part of the decision to accept or refuse a new position.

Deciding to leave your current life for a new one is a major decision that involves real changes. Being fully convinced of your choice greatly increases the chances of a successful expatriation.

It is interesting to note that human beings tend to initially see any change as an obstacle. Our emotions are there to remind us of this – they are our messengers, our guardians.

The first emotion that comes to mind when I think of a situation of change is that of *fear*. Fear is expressed as anxiety, nervousness, concern, even apprehension. Sometimes we even feel these physically, like a feeling of oppression or suffocation in the chest. These emotions, these messages are like a call for help when the individual, as a whole, feels attacked. This announcement of change is like an intrusion into one's comfort zone, and may impact the decisions that you make.

We will therefore seek to reassure ourselves by becoming curious and looking for answers to our questions. These answers will soothe our emotions and reassure us about what we can and cannot (or will not) change.

Looking for answers...

As these changes often take us by surprise, we may want to reassure ourselves or be guided in our first reflections by asking those around us for feedback and getting advice from our loved ones. This is a legitimate and valuable process, but at the end of the day, my personal experience showed that no one can make a better decision for you than you: a unique individual with your own experiences, qualities and instincts.

Thinking back to the young woman I was when I first went abroad, I do not think anyone around me imagined that expat life was going to be a life that was going to suit me so much, that was going to enrich me so much, and that was going to fulfil me so much. I do not think I was even aware of that myself. At the same time, unless I had a crystal ball, how could I or anyone around me have even known?

Faced with the unknown, I just remember trying to project myself into this new adventure by imagining what it might bring me and whether it was the kind of life I wanted for myself at the time. At that moment, I understood that only by taking the risk would I find out the answer to this question. I decided to trust my instincts, to be open to the surprises that life was throwing at me and to live in the moment!

This experience also taught me that you always have the freedom to find a way to make things right. It's true that I often had to rethink my choices because they were not always as good as I thought they would be, but I always found a solution that moved me forward. Being a problem solver, finding solutions also always makes me happy and satisfied! And you know what? It's okay to make mistakes. Mistakes make us grow! They are an important part of the process of thinking and maturing to make effective decisions for ourselves and our family in the future.

We all have our own approach...

Whether you have a specific vision, particular ambitions for your family's future and for yourself, or whether you are just going through the motions of life, there are always times when you have to make choices and think about the consequences of those choices.

Some people may see change as a threat, an obstacle to the future they have envisioned, which can trigger a panicked and negative emotional reaction to making decisions. Other individuals are more pragmatic and adapt to all situations to overcome obstacles and achieve their goals.

Over the years of my expatriation, I have found that everyone has different priorities and that is very respectable. But again, I think that if not clarified and discussed before departure, these priorities can actually lead to the failure of the expatriation adventure.

Women's careers, different scenarios...

Let's take a common example of a wife who chooses to leave her current job to follow her husband.

a. Is the wife's ambition to accompany her husband and potentially discover many new opportunities (or find many closed doors) or to have a similar working life to the one she has now?

b. For some women, work is a matter of life balance before it is a financial issue. In this case, she may be able to find an activity that would satisfy her as much as her former job. Volunteering, for example, is a choice for many expatriate women.

c. For other women, getting back into paid work is essential. What are her chances and rights to find a job in the new host country? What are her possibilities of obtaining a work visa as an expatriate wife? What are the working conditions and costs of childcare facilities, for example? All the questions that arise in this area are numerous and specific to each country.

Getting answers to the essential questions a woman has before she leaves is an important part of making her decision. It is also a way for the woman to feel supported and respected in her decision-making.

In the first chapter I talked about the subject of the wife's career as an important topic to share and clarify with her partner. Here I would like to stress the importance of self-reflection; to be in harmony with yourself and to accept the emotional and financial risks and consequences of changing or giving up your career.

I think that self-reflection is a healthy way to become the only person responsible for one's choices and never to have to blame someone else for the consequences. This means that when one is considering the future they may have in expatriation, self-reflection is essential to make sure they are making the right decisions for themselves.

In expatriation, I can observe that self-reflection comes up frequently, due to the many changes that this lifestyle brings. Adopting a habit of assessing your own behavior can create a pattern of thinking that will be extremely helpful.

An opportunity...

Let me share a sentence that always inspired me: "The world is a place to explore, and it will embrace you if you embrace it." I do not know where I first heard this, but it has stuck with me.

Expatriation is an opportunity for you and your family to grow, to open up to the world and to enjoy it to the fullest. It is an opportunity to live several lives in one.

Often when we talk about age and the passing years, I realize how much I am in harmony with my age; it is perfectly justified by my life, rich in experiences. When I think of all my memories, my encounters, my adventures, 50 years have not been too many to live through!

Living an expatriate life means constantly living in the present; you are eager for new things, you are curious about many things and you are on the lookout for what is going on around you. You catch the opportunities when they present themselves, you know that it may be only a one-off opportunity. Time is often counted, and you do not waste it. You are very active, you take advantage of everything, you like to take initiatives, you like to try new things, you are often very spontaneous and you begin to master situations of change. As expatriates, we are constantly pushed out of our comfort zones, to look for all that life offers us *right now*, and deep down we have to admit that this is what makes us love this life so much every day. This is what makes it all worth it.

The average duration of a placement is between three and five years. Even if a mission can only last three years, we often surprise ourselves with what we are capable of doing and achieving in such a short time frame. Women are each in our own way "bulldozers" who often have only one priority in mind: the wellbeing of our families. It is often the feeling of guilt towards our children that forces us to be particularly active and perform the part of a role model – a feeling that we will come back to in a later chapter.

Here I would like to take a moment to remind all the women who will read this book that we are all capable of going beyond our fears, our prejudices and those of others. Listen to yourself; follow your instincts. Other people's opinions are just opinions. You only have one life and it is yours, so live it to the fullest and make your own choices, only you know what you are capable of. Remember that *you* are the one in control of your own life!

Coaching helped me overcome the fear of a split family...

Even though we made the decision together, as you can probably understand, Alex's transfer to Pakistan had a big emotional impact on me. During his career, Alex had always traveled a lot and was often away during the week. We were used to this rhythm; it was normal and we lived it very well. I think it was the term "split family" that really scared me. I was suddenly afraid that the separation would be like an abandonment, that we would not see each other anymore, that the children would not see their father and that a lack of presence on Alex's part would make us all suffer. Fortunately, things turned out quite differently...

Once the decision was made, we first decided that Alex would take up his post in Pakistan and I would stay in Manila for another six months while the children finished their school year and so all the changes would not happen at the same time. Our family would move to Dubai in the summer and in between Alex would go back and forth on weekends (just writing this still makes me dizzy).

So, we spent six months making the best possible arrangements for the family to be together as often as possible. The commute between the Philippines and Pakistan being long and complicated, Alex, who is extremely family-oriented, always organized the most beautiful weekends in the most beautiful places, often halfway between our two countries. While it was more convenient and also fun to visit new countries, it was also tiring and stressful, especially for the children. It's true that today we have fond memories of this time and the many wonderful discoveries we made, but I remember that after those few months of constant traveling, moving and staying in hotels, we just wanted to stay at home and avoid taking a plane.

To come back to the emotional impact that this transfer had on me, it is important to mention that at that time, as my husband's promotion was not yet official, I was not allowed to share my future plans with my friends in Manila. For me, a fairly transparent person, it was an extra weight on my shoulders to have to keep this situation secret.

Despite Alex's supportive attitude, I suddenly felt lonely. I needed someone to share my feelings with. I wanted to be helped by someone outside of the situation. Someone neutral, empathetic and non-judgmental. I felt I needed someone to talk to, someone I could trust, who would listen to me with a professional ear. So that's when I called my friend Maud, who is a certified life coach.

A life coach is a professional who will guide you in your personal development to design the future you want for yourself and your loved ones. Just as you would hire a sports or nutrition coach to help you achieve your goals in these areas, a life coach will help you analyze your emotions, their messages and implement techniques to make your life the one you want. In my case, I was looking for an expert to support me in my loneliness, my lack of orientation and to help me come out of this situation peacefully and at peace with myself.

As an expat herself, I knew Maud would understand me. From the outset, I noticed that in spite of our friendship, the sessions were extremely professional and I immediately felt a sense of trust. From the very first session we clarified why I came to coaching and what my short- and long-term objectives were. We also discussed my feelings and how I would like to feel at the end of this journey. From the start, Maud's questions were pertinent – insightful reflections on what she observed in my words, my silences and my actions. Everything was about me; she was fully present with me and at no point did she try to give me advice based on her own experience. Maud made me seek the answers to the questions I had within myself – this was a fascinating journey that made me grow amazingly internally. Thanks to this guidance and personal development work, my six months of transition went smoothly. What a relief!

This coaching experience has been invaluable to me. I have always liked to see *life as an expat woman* as a continuous course in personal development, life lessons with important ups and downs. Sometimes you are strong, sometimes you are not so strong. Even if sometimes it takes an effort to ask for help, we must remember that it is a human need. It is not a sign of weakness, but rather a sign of strength. Accepting our weaknesses and responding to them can lead more quickly to progress and success.

My coaching experience with Maud has really been essential to my continued growth and development. Asking for help was really rewarded by enabling me to continue my expat life with more strength and resilience.

If at this moment of my life I had the chance to discover what coaching was, coaching remains a tool among others. Personally, I have to admit that I had a lot of pleasure going through this transition by discovering what coaching was and the outcomes that can be obtained through this personal development work. However, it is true that there are as many ways to get help as there are human beings; once again, it is a very personal path.

Encounters...

The success of my expatriate life is also largely the result of the encounters, friendships and relationships I have developed and the bonds that still unite us today. This life experience with my friend Maud is a perfect example. We met in Mexico, developed a friendship and made memories. When Maud left for new adventures, we stayed in touch, I continued to follow her career and her professional activities. As soon as I needed help, I thought of her, her job, I wanted to try coaching. I then called her from Manila for her professional skills.

Following my coaching experience with Maud and observing the positive impact it had on my life, I became very interested in this profession and the qualifications required to be a good life coach.

From the beginning, I knew that a career as a life coach would suit me. I am passionate about other people; I am curious and empathetic. I also know that regardless of language, culture or background, people tend to connect with me because of my natural positivity, energy, creativity and even humor. I hope that is coming across in this book, connecting with you and supporting you along your journey.

I would like to take a moment here to share one of my objectives in writing this book. I would like to thank each of these people who have a special place in my life. I am filled with gratitude for you all and the special encounters I have made before and during my expat life. They have made me the person I am today, and I am incredibly grateful. I hope that each of you will recognize yourself as one of those who has contributed to my life.

Nanette...

My friend Nanette likes to mention that when she arrived in the Philippines, I made her appreciate the country and the culture in which we lived. Over time, she naturally felt connected and integrated to this country after a challenging start. Nanette came from Hong Kong and the way of life in these two cities required a real effort to adapt.

Nanette was working in Hong Kong and when she arrived in Manila, she wanted to find a professional activity. Together, we often discussed her ambitions, her strengths and the opportunities that this country could offer her. Nanette eventually worked for a modern art gallery and launched exhibitions of young Filipino artists. The exhibitions gave these artists the chance to become known locally and internationally. Through these successful exhibitions, Nanette was able to find the activity she needed at the time to fulfill herself and make her experience in the Philippines a rich and rewarding one.

I was happy for her. I realized how much being there for Nanette and watching her transformation from a tough start in Manila to being successful in her career also made me happy. I liked the concept and I liked the idea of potentially being there for other women.

This encounter with Nanette happened at the same time as my work with Maud. I then realized that what Maud was doing with me was strangely similar to what I was doing instinctively with Nanette.

When I gradually realized that my skills and strengths would be an asset in this career, I was very excited that my life experiences of the past 25 years would also be useful in understanding other women who were preparing for or already living in expatriation. Coaching would also keep me in touch and bring me into contact with other people from all over the world, people who were like me, with whom I had something in common. This is exactly the feeling I have always been looking for, it is what has always nourished and energized me in my expatriations.

From this awareness, I have learned to listen and be present for my friends (when support is required) and for my clients in a professional way. Short-term results are replaced by long-term results – coaching is so powerful! I've continually developed through ongoing training and my passion in this field keeps on growing.

I continue to be coached myself, and the writing and publishing of this book is the best proof of that: I would never have dared to embark on such an adventure if I had not had faith in coaching and in Mindy, my book coach. Too many obstacles would have held me back, I would never have known how to structure my work, manage my time and get through each step to make this book happen. Knowing first-hand what results you get from coaching, I was confident that Mindy would guide me to the realization of my dream! Thank you, Mindy, for this amazing journey!

From my first steps in coaching, I knew I wanted to help spouses and mothers of expatriates who are going through a transition, a change. This is indeed my expertize. I have done it all and am now here to help you do it too.

Reflections...

To help identify what is important for you in the expatriation life, I invite you to reflect on these questions:

- What would help you know if moving abroad is the right decision for you?

- What happens when you follow your instinct?

- What is your ambition for yourself and for your family?

CHAPTER

FIVE

Expatriation can lead to a better life

Expatriation often comes as a job promotion. It is usually therefore excellent news and a statistically great career move for an employee who receives this offer. Financially, an expatriation is also often an opportunity to offer the family privileged living conditions: children will likely have access to international school, housing will certainly be subsidized or free to compensate for the cost of living, and health insurance is often included. The bonus or hardship allowance enables you to enjoy the country you are living in to the fullest, and often gives you the opportunity to take wonderful trips to see the surrounding area and explore your new home. It is also an opportunity to save money and invest for your future. For example, many expats save for a nice retirement or to provide a good education for their children.

Quality versus quantity...

Expatriation is also an opportunity to enjoy a very good quality of life. In many countries, you can choose to have help at home, which gives you more time to spend with your family and friends, or to do things that you would not have the time to do if you had to take care of everything on your own.

We have always lived in emerging countries, where it is common to have help at home. I have always seen this form of employment to be a positive exchange that benefits both the locals and my family.

Let's not forget that the salary we pay to our employees will allow them to support their families. Every penny is necessary for them, so knowing what they will earn is a priority for them.

I remember coming across expat families who were surprised to have the question of salary and holidays in the first questions of the interview. Although I understand that this may seem awkward on the part of the employee, I think it is important to understand their life and their needs. The conditions that will make them choose to work for your family may not be the same as those you might think of.

If seeing an employee leave can feel like a betrayal from an expatriate family's point of view, I think it is important not to take this departure personally but to eventually put yourself in that person's shoes and try to understand the underlying reasons/needs for this decision.

Personally, what I appreciate most about having this valuable help is that I can really choose which tasks I want to keep and delegate those that do not give me any gratification. This freedom has allowed me to have a lot of time for myself and also to be very available for my children when they need it. This is a real luxury that I think is recognized and appreciated by most expatriate parents.

I can never thank enough all the nannies who have worked with us, for being so kind and dedicated to my children and to our family. Their good mood, dedication and flexibility have always been part of the positive atmosphere in our house.

I was always lucky to have wonderful help at home. Julie has been with us since our first day in the Philippines, and until today, eight years later, here in Dubai. She takes care of everything in the house. My children can see that and have also learned to be extremely respectful and grateful for everything Julie does for them. She has seen them grow up and also feels very attached to them. They have also developed their own relationship, I often hear them laughing, getting organized, and this bond is important for Julie who has left her own two children in her home country. If our helper transforms our daily life, we must never forget how complicated hers is and the frequent and serious sacrifices she is making to support her own family.

Constantin always tells me that the day he goes to university, he will take Julie with him. Julie cooks like a Michelin star chef, and has taken his diet very seriously. Constantin is very dedicated to go-karting and needs a special diet. For seven years now she has taken care to always cook the exact food and quantity that "her boy," as she calls Constantin, is allowed. He is extremely grateful to her.

I think the secret to keeping our precious helpers around is also to treat them as we would like to be treated, with respect and courtesy, like a member of our family.

This help gave me, what is in my opinion, the greatest luxury of expatriation: *time*. Time to have the freedom to do what you want to, when you want to. If at the beginning of expatriation, you feel like you have been presented with a blank sheet of paper, a fresh start and a new life, very soon you will begin to draw the life you have always dreamed of.

Habits that will take your expat experience to the next level...

As I left for West Africa 25 years ago, I did not know what my tomorrow would be like, and this was destabilizing and disorientating. Now, I wake up every morning with a real sense of excitement to be able to use my days to do all the things I have decided and organized to do. To live them to the fullest exactly as I want. At first, I was a little unsettled to have such freedom in my daily life, but now I am so grateful to be completely in control of my life. This is something that I have only managed to do through practicing and perfecting a few habits that are essential to life as an expatriate.

Another objective with this book is to show as many women who have been invited to experience expatriation as possible that this thrilling and pleasurable adventure really is accessible to all who wish to seek it for themselves. By being curious, by meeting people, by being grateful for what you are experiencing, and by being patient and tolerant, you can have a successful expatriation. Having said that, if you've ever agreed to go abroad, it is because you're already curious, curious to see what's going on elsewhere.

Curiosity...

My curiosity has always been my ally and my driving force. Thanks to this curiosity, my self-confidence has grown and allowed me to live a number of extraordinary experiences. My curiosity encouraged me to reach out to others, to explore the culture of every host country and to understand everything that was happening around me on a daily basis. This curiosity first helped me to get closer to each country and a fortiori to integrate more quickly.

The Philippines was my second expatriation on the Asian continent since I had lived in Indonesia a few years earlier. What I have learned about the Indonesian culture did not help me to understand the Philippines' history and civilization. Two very different cultures due to two distinct historical pasts. When I arrived in the Philippines, I was quickly surprised that only the elders still speak Spanish but the younger generations only speak English. For those who had the chance to go to school, their level of English is actually very high due to the influence of the Americans in the country.

I found Filipinos to be extremely hospitable, religious, kind, devoted, optimistic, they never say no and will always smile despite the heavy and painful past of their country's history. These are some Filipino traits that often leave foreigners perplexed. Personally, I was really curious to understand the history of the Philippines and the impact of this past on their culture, their behavior and their language.

The Museum Volunteers of the Philippines (MVP) understood the importance of sharing their history in order to encourage a better understanding of the country and its people's philosophy. The MVP is still organizing a school year course covering major historical events in the Philippines. These topics are often presented by Filipinos who themselves lived through these periods or who are direct descendants of the people who made Philippines' history. Topics cover key episodes from the pre-colonial period up to the modern day, and this course has always been very popular with expatriate women to better understand and immerse themselves in their host country.

This kind of integration and understanding of historical events that shape a current society is very important in expatriation. Your efforts to learn the history and past struggles of the host country will be appreciated and will contribute to an overall integration into the country and connection to its people.

Social life...

Speaking the language, understanding and living the culture in which you settle is also a way to get closer to the locals and to be enriched by this experience. For me, connection with people is essential. Whether they are expatriates or locals, building a social life has always been absolutely essential to me – it is a requirement for my survival.

In Mexico we were lucky enough to be fully immersed in local Mexican life. We chose to live in a residence mainly inhabited by Mexicans and our children went to school with their children. Our friends were mostly Mexican; we were invited to their family parties in their family *haciendas*.

When I arrived in the Philippines, I was still so attached to Mexican culture that I immediately joined an extraordinary group of Latin expatriate women in Manila: "*club de damas latinas*." It just so happened that the first event in September was the Mexican National Day luncheon, and I decided to open my house to host the luncheon and I received 60 Spanish-speaking women in my house. For the record, it was one of the most beautiful luncheons I have ever hosted, but more importantly, I was now a part of this group. I had made myself known, I had taken the first step to go to this group that attracted me. Among these women, I made friendships that lasted the time of my expatriation to the Philippines, some of whom I am still in contact with today. Of course, you may not meet your best friend at the first lunch, but the important thing is to seize the opportunities when they arise and to develop your social network little by little.

Patience and tolerance...

No one person adapts to a country the exact same way. I have learned over time that patience is a necessary virtue for expatriation. First of all, this is because at the beginning, nothing works the way you want it to, especially because you often arrive with your own cultural criteria that may well be very different from your new reality. Like any expat, I have experienced my moments of frustration and also moments of loneliness. Even though these frustrations may be caused by issues that seem irrelevant to other people, in your heightened emotional state they can be the thing that tips you over the edge. If at first these situations are discouraging, with time you learn to anticipate them, and later laugh about them.

I cannot tell you how many times I have arrived at a supermarket and not found what I was looking for, either because the product was out of stock or discontinued. In these moments, I have seen many of my peers become frustrated and overwhelmed, even by such a small inconvenience. I remember when Nesquik was out of stock in our local supermarket in the Philippines – many kids and adults alike were in an uproar – it was a surprisingly emotional affair!

Over time, I have learned to step back from these situations and take them as they come; adopting a flexible attitude and viewing such frustrations as nothing more than additional life experience rather than as a personal attack.

Even if I like to say that expat life is a gift for me, I admit that every moment is not a cherished one either... I know that when we, expats, talk about our past experiences and reflect on our good and bad moments, we laugh about them and we are even more grateful, and happy to have left the bad ones behind us!

This reflection reminds me of a special moment in the Philippines. For all the women who have lived in Manila, I think they will agree with me that until you have had your gifts wrapped at the Landmark, a shopping mall, you have not yet fully immersed yourself in this city and in the Filipino culture. It is a rite of initiation! The wrapping of a gift is done in stages, and each stage by a different employee; one will cut the paper, one will wrap the sides, another the top and so on. It is a painfully slow process; a real lesson in patience and self-control. Despite your growing impatience, you know that it would be extremely rude and completely unacceptable to lose your temper!

The attitude of gratitude...

I know that many women like to keep a gratitude journal. Every day they write down what has been positive for them, no matter how small. It's also a way of reflecting on their own life and getting into the habit of appreciating each happy moment and making the experience more and more positive. While I have never done this myself, I can imagine that it would be an encouraging process; taking things day by day and learning to stop and appreciate the happy moments – things that you are grateful for – in times when you feel uncertain, afraid or like nothing is going right. It is an important step in feeling grounded in a country.

There is an extremely positive and productive energy in expat groups. By joining the various groups, you can really fill your days, weeks and weekends with activities and people that inspire you and bring you joy.

Our real responsibility in joining these groups is our attitude and commitment. As expats, we know that we can quickly feel lonely and unhappy and so we prefer to avoid people who don't transmit that same energy. You need to keep a positive attitude so that you attract others that do the same. However, if you are feeling down, don't stay alone; talk to others, ask for help, you will find that others are currently there or have been there and will be happy to share their contacts, their solutions. The only advice I could give you in this book is to take charge of your life, you are really the only one responsible for adapting and immersing yourself as best you can.

I found my place in this journey...

Over the years I have really felt that my life has gradually become more and more rewarding, exciting and thrilling. By trusting my instinct and curiosity, I focused on what interested me and made me happy.

This active and open-minded attitude has always given me the confidence to remain open to the opportunities that each country has to offer. Learning what I had undertaken in a first country was often no longer relevant in the next, and I had to start again. This gave me the opportunity to try many things, and I must admit that I still love it.

When I lived in Africa, the price of gold and silver was very affordable. At that time, I already liked to design jewelry and I had started working with a Senegalese jeweler named Touba. Touba had a small workshop on the side of a barely-paved road. It was around 20 meters squared, lit by one or two neon lights, and a few display cases on a dirt floor. You could see that he had been working for many years on his beautiful jeweler's workbench, well-rounded so that he could rest his arms comfortably.

With only a few tools and a blowtorch, it was amazing to see what he could achieve with so little material. I loved going to see him, picking up simple but beautiful pieces, and talking with him. I learned a lot from him, not only about jewelry but also about traditions and the Muslim culture in Africa. Cotonou was predominantly Catholic, however, I remember that at the time of Ramadan, as is traditional, people around me were offering a sheep to their Muslim friends when they felt appreciation for them.

I was happy to do the same for Touba. He would share this sheep with his friends and family. Touba is one of the marvelous encounters that made me love my years in Cotonou so much.

When you spend lots of time in a place, you naturally develop relationships with the people who are part of your daily life. Whether it's the fruit vendor, the bookseller, the baker or anyone else. At the beginning, it's a smile, then two or three words. Together, we were talking about their life, often about their family, I was simply interested in them. As time passes, we gradually get closer to this country and its inhabitants who welcome us so warmly. A connection like the one I found in Touba, I've found in every destination. Unfortunately, these are the people you will lose when you leave the country, but I could never forget that they formed a part of my life during the years I spent living in their country.

When I arrived in Jakarta, I went from a small city on the west coast of Africa to an Asian megalopolis. I naturally gave up jewelry-making and moved on without regret. It was part of another life, another experience. In expatriation I think it is important not to compare your present life with what you have experienced elsewhere. I feel that each experience deserves to be lived in its own right.

Expatriation is a dynamic way of life...

In 25 years of expatriation, I have become a mother of two. Until the birth of Constantin, I had never held a baby in my arms for the simple reason that I had never had small children around me. The experience of motherhood was therefore totally new to me, and has been a fundamental part of my journey, of how I found my place. Despite the geographical distance from my friends and family, I was lucky enough to naturally quickly gain confidence and felt extremely happy and serene with my new little family.

It was only when I arrived in Indonesia in 2003 that I was really able to start communicating via the internet, email and Skype. Connectivity was way faster than in Africa and despite the time difference between me and my friends and family, we could communicate easily. Thanks to this new form of communication, we all felt less distant from each other, which drastically changed the isolation theme for expatriates.

I was happy to realize that as the years went by, I had established a new life; my own life. I had created my new bubble in which I was more than happy. I had a lot of responsibilities again, both on a personal and family level. I felt like I was really in control of my life, or at least in control of what I could control. I felt fulfilled and really felt like I was in the right place at the right time.

This, I understand, is not an experience unique to me. Many of my expat friends have similarly found fulfilment in their nomadic lives. Not long ago I asked my friend Caroline how she spent her days in her new country of expatriation and she answered with a sentence that I found so beautiful, "I am busy being happy."

As I write these lines I realize how much pleasure (and nostalgia) I get from looking back and reflecting on the different stages of my expatriate life. I have a good sense of how things have worked out and realize how much life has rewarded my efforts. All the opportunities I have experienced woke up facets of my personality that were previously latent. I have accumulated positive and very rewarding experiences that have made me grow and become the person I am today.

In my case, being an expatriate was to leave a life that was probably all mapped out and stable to seek a life rich in experience and adventure. It was all worth it.

Thank you, Alex!

Expatriation is your opportunity to live your life the way you want...

Expatriate life is an opportunity to take the time to do what you usually don't have time to do. While some people get bored on holiday, others may need a holiday after their holidays as they get stuck into so many activities. The same goes for expatriate life: what you decide to do with it is again a matter of choice, attitude and personality.

It is interesting to see how a small change in attitude can totally change life experiences. Living and working away from home can be a real challenge, some challenges and obstacles that cannot be avoided; however, it's in our hands to choose the attitude we take to this situation. We can decide to see it as an opportunity to learn something new or to be the victim of these frustrations. This change of attitude will make all the difference!

Believe me, expatriation transforms. It makes us grow and open up to others! The more we travel the world, the more we feel connected, belonging to this world that we are taming more and more! You start to feel good everywhere you go and above all you connect easily with people of all nationalities wherever you are. How many times have we found people from nationalities and cultures we know, with whom we can communicate in their language, use their expressions, tell them that we know their country or even their city. This direct contact with people is all part of the magic of expat life!

Our experiences enrich us and develop our self-confidence. As I said earlier, our only responsibility is to decide where to start. Each expatriate has their own pace, it is not a race and there are no winners. There is no competition, there is no sequence to follow. In expatriation, you mingle with people of all ages who simply have the same interest as you do at the same time. Age is not an obstacle in expatriation.

I like to remember my bridge games on Mondays in Brazil. I have always loved card games, and in Brazil I wanted to join a group of women bridge players. Every Monday, taking turns to be at each other's houses, we met between eight and 15 women aged between 25 and 65. The most experienced ones patiently taught us the rules of the game and very quickly our Monday meetings became unmissable; friendly, warm and filled with laughter.

Again, great friendships with women who for some had already walked the path that we, as young expats, were setting out upon. We enjoyed listening to their experiences and their advice, we liked their stories which were often similar to those we could have heard during a family reunion.

If some had their children in boarding school, others were celebrating the end of their children's studies or were already starting to organize their elders' weddings. At the same time, we, the youngest, were starting to have children! These were differences that in fact brought us closer together. Being part of such groups, feeling that we give as much as we receive is also a way to feel as if we are valued and important.

Once again, this experience shows how important it is to trust your instincts and leave all your prejudices behind. You may be surprised!

Be open to new emotions, get out of your comfort zone and live fully this adventure that is offered to you!

Reflections...

To help identify what is valuable for you in the expatriation life, I invite you to reflect on these questions:

- Apart from moving countries, what might be the greatest change for you if you were/are living an expat life?

- What impact do you foresee this change having on your life?

- What one experience shared so far resonates most with you?

CHAPTER

SIX

Expatriate life is an opportunity to open your mind to the world

Once you start to be interested in your new country, the country and the people will be equally interested in you.

I would like to start this chapter with a scene from African life. Imagine the biggest market in West Africa: it is in Benin, in Cotonou, it is the Dantokpa market.

All around you there is bartering and bickering over the sale of second-hand clothes and fabrics, the smell of humans, overripe fruits, wood fires, gas from all the mopeds drunk on two-stroke petrol. The most pungent of all is the smell of goats, the sacred animal in the Muslim religion.

All the women in the region are dressed in "*boubou*," the traditional African loincloth. They are beautiful, and it suits them well. The fabrics are so-called Wax, which originally came from Holland. The prices of these Waxes vary according to the quality of the fabrics and the printed patterns. Historically, each pattern means something; it conveys a message. It was a real language used by women: a wish, a message addressed to their husband or to another woman. Each drawing, even a simple one, has an important meaning, like everything else in Africa. Africans have an extremely visual language. They speak as they see; everything is a description of images. Like life in Africa, it is beautifully simple.

On each *boubou* there is a drawing and an explanatory sentence. One of the most popular designs is a drawing of a bird cage, with the door open and two birds flying away.

The printed message is: "you go out, I go out" which means: husband, be careful, if you are unfaithful, I will be too.

Of course, no one expects foreigners to dress like African women. On the other hand, to be interested in them, their customs and values and to ask them questions is a way of gaining their respect and showing that foreigners who come to live in their country are interested in their culture.

Cultural empathy...

I must acknowledge that before leaving for Africa, I did not inform myself about the habits and customs of Benin and its region. I was young, in love and was really going on an adventure without asking myself any questions or thinking carefully.

However, as I mentioned before, little by little, I learned to anticipate my surprise and transform it into curiosity. Today, whether the experience is good or bad, this curiosity stimulates me to understand and discover more things around me. If those experiences have made me grow a lot on a personal level, it has also transformed my life. Having the chance to constantly discover new cultures is a part of my expat life that I really appreciate. I never had thought about the culture shock or the emotions it would trigger in me. When I began my expat adventure, I went from surprise to surprise, my emotions were overwhelmed. Now, before I move to a new country, I inform and prepare myself more so that the shock is less abrupt and the adjustment is easier and smoother when I arrive.

Going out there...

At the time I arrived in Africa, I remember that we young expatriate women were very active.

I would like to remind you that in 1998, there was still very little information on the internet. To find out what was going on around us, there was only one way: going out there and seeing for ourselves! My first blessing was to arrive in a country where French (my mother tongue) was spoken – this was one less obstacle to navigate. My second fortune was to be surrounded by Lebanese people, an extremely welcoming community. The Lebanese are settled all over the West African coast because of the climate, the language and the opportunities to develop their businesses.

Alex was responsible for his company for all of the West African market, from Ghana to Congo. He traveled a lot, so if I did not go with him, I was often home alone. I remember that when our Lebanese friends heard that Alex was going to travel, they would call me to invite me to contact them if I needed anything. This kindness and knowing that someone cared about me, often helped me to overcome the long evenings spent alone with my Labrador as my only company in my big house in Africa. I quickly understood the importance of surrounding myself with friends and creating a second family. This was essential for my happiness and development.

Let's remember that loneliness at the beginning of an expatriation can be difficult. As with many new situations at the beginning of an expatriation, you do not know what to expect and you do not know who to talk to. We do not yet have our first friends and although our family and friends at home care about us, they are not there to understand our own and unique situation.

Being part of the community...

While there are identical ways that can be recommended to facilitate meeting people in each country, I believe the truth is that meeting people is really a matter of luck; being in the right place at the right time.

You do not always meet your best friends at the beginning of your stay. I remember that in Africa, one of Alex's work colleagues and his wife took good care of me at the beginning of our stay, but very soon the relationship became toxic and invasive, and our discussions made me sad and even scared. I soon decided that I would rather get away from these people.

By going to the beach at weekends, joining activity groups, chatting with expats I met, opportunities to meet potential friends began to present themselves. From dinners to parties, we started to have a very active and fun social life. In general, in expatriation, people host at home often. On the one hand because we often have help and on the other hand it is the spirit of expatriation: spontaneity, sharing, simplicity, meeting, discovering, having fun and enjoying every moment! There is even a name for this type of gathering: "potluck party." This strong spirit of conviviality can also be found in countries where the foreign community is as limited as the places to go out. All the chances you will have to meet others means that you will find your people – but they may not be the first friends you make, so you have to keep looking.

Eventually, we'll find our place...

Alex and I had really made our mark. Most of my Lebanese friends were working, as they were not expatriates and often helped their husbands in their businesses. So, it was with my few expat friends that I went to discover the markets (like Daktopa), the local craftsmen and the gems of this region. However, it did not take us long to make the full tour – it was not a big city. The town center was limited to a drugstore, a bookstore, and two mini supermarkets. There were no clothes shops, so instead we bought the fabric and had copies made of our clothes brought back from Europe.

As you might be able to tell, my first expatriate experience was a culture shock. I really had to get out of my comfort zone and push myself to avoid the urge to jump on the first plane and get back to my well-organized life in Switzerland.

Giving back a bit of what life offered me...

In Geneva, I was working in a communication agency. One of our clients was a Swiss humanitarian organization for whom we had rebranded its image and communication. By chance, this same organization was also present in Cotonou. The director, Roxanne, was a very empathic Canadian lady. I contacted her, told her I had just arrived in Cotonou, and I was interested to see what they were doing in Africa.

I asked her if I could accompany her on one of her missions. She took me along, but very quickly, I understood that being a humanitarian in the field is a vocation. It is a job that requires real psychological and physical strength. I was disturbed by what I saw, and I felt that I could not stay idle, so I suggested to Roxanne that I might work on their communication development and fundraising to do my part. In all the countries I have lived in, I have always been able to find an activity that allowed me to give back to the country and the people – to return a few of the favors that it gave me.

For my family and myself, Africa has always been a very special continent. Together, Alex and I discovered many countries and returned there to holiday with our children. There is an energy, a light and a smell on this continent that moves me every time I set foot on these lands. Even though I am always nostalgic to relive the best moments spent in a country, I know that I would not want to do a second expatriation in a country where I have already lived. So, I never imagined going back to Africa, but the time I spent there gave me a love for the place that has lasted long after I left for a new adventure. I still love to travel there and make my children discover this wonderful continent.

Studying online...

As activities were quite limited in Africa, I quickly found that I wanted to occupy myself intellectually. Having so many free hours at my disposal presented an opportunity to resume my studies. A cousin, who was an expatriate in Vietnam, had graduated from an English-based university (The Open University) and what she described seemed to fit the bill: a flexible timetable, where internet connectivity was not a problem and where my level of English allowed me to follow the courses. I was looking for a university in Switzerland or France, but I must admit that in 2000, The Open University was really the pioneer in online studies. Students received modules that we printed out and studied, then sent back our essays and we could ask our professors questions by email. There was no such thing as a visual conference. Communication was not instantaneous at all.

Our only obligation was to go to England twice a year to The Open University campus for a week's seminar followed by final exams to be taken on site. That was how I got my first online degree. Since then, online studies have evolved and I have taken great advantage of this system to continue studying the areas that interest me.

If today, in the era of COVID-19, studying and communicating online is becoming a norm, I can promise you that up until not so long ago, it was quite avant-garde.

Lost in translation...

I remember an anecdote that always makes me smile. I was taking tennis lessons with an American girl, and one day I told her that I would be away for the next two weeks because I was going to England to take exams for my university degree. She replied, "break a leg!" Not knowing the English expression, I understood only the literal meaning of this saying, and needless to say, I was shocked! It was only when I came back home and told Alex the story that I understood that it was an English expression which meant "good luck."

This is obviously just one of many anecdotes and I think we have all experienced misinterpretations as expatriates which in retrospect make us laugh.

Soul searching...

In chapter two, I talked about the different phases of expatriation. I mentioned the first phase as the "honeymoon phase." In my experience, this period ends naturally when you start to question yourself and ask yourself what your role is in this new country, what the meaning of your life is. You are then a bit disoriented and you often need to question yourself. It is the time to realign your life with what you want in your present situation.

This is also one of the gifts of expat life: you have the choice to do what makes you happy. A priceless opportunity that, I would like to remind you, might not have arisen if you had not had the courage to move abroad.

Sitting down and taking the time to self-reflect and be introspective is an opportunity to identify your needs, your goals, your interests. It is also a chance to discover and take advantage of the opportunities specific to the country in which you will spend a few years. It is a phase often described as a "crisis phase" of identification, because we often go through it alone. Although we may have already made friends with new people, this is a time when we may want to have a more formal discussion in order to get some specific outcomes for ourselves.

It is precisely in a case like this that coaching sessions can be of great support.

Coaching is a tool that will allow you to be accompanied and guided in your reflection. It is my job as a coach to get you to think and find a way to change what is not working or even to improve something that is already working. My role is to bring to light what you cannot see for yourself by getting you to see the situation from a different perspective than the one you have today.

From caterpillar to butterfly...

When we arrive in new countries with our background and experiences, our behaviors and habits will automatically need to change due to our new environment. Although you can keep some pattern to settling down in two different environments, it is important not to compare two places and to start to develop new habits. The habits that I had put in place in Mexico, I could not repeat in the Philippines. In Mexico, I really enjoyed my independence. I truly enjoyed taking my car and going down to the center of Mexico City to visit an exhibition in a museum, have lunch with a friend or go shopping. I loved my "me days" in such a warm and beautiful city. When I arrived in the Philippines, I realized that I wouldn't find the same freedom. The traffic was horribly heavy, even worse than in Mexico City. Even though the company had provided us with a driver in Manila, my life was mainly spent in my neighborhood.

In order to blend in as quickly as possible in my new countries, I have always tried not to let my past hold me back, letting change happen while keeping what is essential for me: my values. My values are what make me happy, satisfied and content with my life.

I believe that we tend to lose track of our life when we lose the sense of our values. Values are very personal; we are not born with values, we learn them through life. However, they determine the way you want to live, bring up your kids and maybe work.

Although these beginnings are often chaotic, I know that the most important thing for me is to face my anxieties and fears in order to remain authentic and present to those I love. I want to give off positive energy so that everyone around me feels loved and part of this transition, which, once it is over, will unite us and make us stronger.

Reflections...

To help identify what factors will be a challenge for you in expatriate life, I invite you to reflect on these questions:

- What do you expect to be the greatest challenges for you as an expatriate?

- What are your experiences of discovering a new culture or a new environment?

- What resilience or resources would support you towards this transition?

CHAPTER SEVEN

The diversity of the expat life is so rich

I wished for something different...

From Brazil, we moved to Mexico. Two countries geographically close, but culturally so different. From the beginning I sensed that I would have to rethink myself and recreate a life totally different from what I knew.

During the exploratory trip to Mexico, I had insisted to Alex that we live in the center of Mexico City. I really wanted to live in the center of a capital city. I wanted to experience the excitement and frenzy of a big city, to enjoy the restaurants, the cinemas, the theatres, the museums, all the things I had missed in the last few years. I felt that my years in Africa, Indonesia and Brazil had really taken me away from all my references in movies, music and more, and I really wanted to reconnect with all of that.

At that time, my dream would have been to be transferred to New York or Hong Kong; two positions that Alex could have obtained, but my husband has always liked to live in a house, to be surrounded by greenery and above all not to be far from the equator.

So, we stayed in Mexico City during our exploratory trip. Mexico City is a very green city and I knew that many of Alex's colleagues and their families had moved into very nice houses in neighborhoods that I liked. Sadly, at that time, the market was not in our favor and we only visited old houses in which everything had to be upgraded. As the days went by, the agent had nothing to offer us in town.

Our relocation agent knew we played golf and suggested we visit a residence that was 40km from the city center but 20 minutes from Alex's office. I don't need to tell you how I felt, but Alex convinced me to give it a chance. Arms crossed in the car, I saw this countryside scroll by and the city fade away.

After a 40-minute drive, we finally arrived at our destination. Eduardo, the agent who was going to show us some properties, was waiting for us with a big smile and that classic Mexican warm attitude, one of the things that makes them so unique in my eyes. Alex was a bit embarrassed and seeing that I hadn't smiled once the whole way, asked me again if I wanted to turn back. I remember answering Alex, saying that Eduardo seemed so friendly that we could quickly visit two houses, just so as to be polite.

When I arrived at Los Encinos, I was immediately thrown into the real Mexico. At the entrance of the compound, there was a lovely little church made of traditional stones, the entrance was built with natural grey stones, the walls were washed in ochre colors and the security guards at the entrance made me feel secure – a detail that is important in Mexico.

At the time, I did not dare admit to myself that I felt butterflies waking up inside me as I was already beginning to imagine myself living in this little corner of paradise.

From then on, it only took me three houses to find the one that made me forget everything I had initially wished for in this new expatriation.

I would not be surprised if the elements of my story (told in a different context of course) remind many people of a moment in their own unique expatriate experience. At this precise moment, I did a 180, this time I listened to my heart and not my head. I want to believe that we have all found ourselves in the same situation at some point in our expatriate adventure.

It was time for me to accept certain frustrations, keeping an open mind and flexibility. Staying positive, accepting things sometimes reluctantly and having to transform this new situation into the best thing that can happen to us and our families.

The richness of expatriate life certainly keeps your mind young, flexible and constantly evolving!

I am sure you won't be surprised to hear that our expatriation to Mexico will remain in all four of our hearts as an exceptional memory.

Let's adapt to the new situation...

My expat life plan before Mexico was that our children would benefit from being schooled from A to Z in English in the international schools of the cities in which we would live. We had made a good start in Brazil. Constantin was at the international school in Curitiba. He was very happy there, spoke English and Portuguese, at school and with his friends, and the language of the house was always French. Ideal scenario for me!

When we arrived in Mexico, the fact that we could not find a house in the center of Mexico City made us rethink our choice of school. We decided to prioritize the quality of life rather than the school. This choice was motivated by the fact that the children were still young and that we were only planning to stay in Mexico for three years. Miraflores, the local Mexican school, was five minutes away from our house, the American school was 40 minutes away on the highway.

We decided that it would be a good opportunity for the children to learn Spanish and that they would be reintegrated into the English international program the next time we moved. A choice that fit the phase of life we were going through. Now that the children have grown up and the choice of school and curriculum is more important to us and to the children's immediate future, we think differently and the choice of school obviously takes priority over the choice of home location.

Los Encinos was a residence where mainly Mexicans lived and so, Miraflores, a very well-known school in Mexico had opened a campus on our doorstep. We thought it was a chance for our children to study Spanish in optimal conditions. We were probably the only non-Spanish speaking expatriate family who had our children in this traditional Catholic Mexican school.

However, this choice of school was actually also the catalyst for our successful integration in Mexico!

It was a small school: the families all lived nearby and the mums were very involved in school life. Parents were regularly invited to breakfasts and the students prepared many presentations which we looked forward to attending.

By dropping Constantin off at school every morning and being present at all the events, the mothers quickly responded to my smiles. Yet I was the real outsider for them: I did not speak Spanish, and I had an expatriate background that intrigued them. I could very easily have been left out. On the contrary, I was very lucky because from the beginning they made the effort to speak to me in English and to include my children in all the playdates and birthdays that took place outside the school. Their welcoming attitude motivated me to learn Spanish, to be present and to be able to communicate easily with them quickly.

They appreciated my commitment to immerse myself in their country. Mexicans are very proud of their country and are very patriotic. They like to share their culture, they like us to feel at home. This welcome won us over from the start and it is true that Alex and I have always tried to embrace the diversity of our expat life! For all these reasons, Mexico has become our second home.

Schools are great places to meet new friends...

The school is often a great place to meet new people. If you are expats with young kids, I really encourage all parents to take advantage of this opportunity.

In international schools, parent/teacher associations are groups of parent volunteers whose role is to help families immerse themselves in their new environment. These associations are open to all nationalities and I promise you that each participant can make a difference in their own way. I was always very impressed to see how much these mothers engaged themselves to achieve often extraordinary events that had a strong impact on the lives of the students and parents at the school.

It is true that this may seem to be a mentality particular to English speakers, however all nationalities are very welcome and the mix of culture, skills and creativity leads to some extraordinary events. I often think of graduation parties in Manila, where many mothers had spectacular and very original ideas that could have really inspired the biggest event planners!

As a result of the number of nationalities in the international schools, the range of activities is naturally very diverse and the quality of the teaching is often of a very high standard.

I remember how popular activities organized by school were. The highly competitive sports within the school or between international schools on the same continent are extremely important gatherings for many students and parents. The school then becomes a real second family for many of these expatriates.

I do understand that not all expats want to live such a close life with the school or with groups, but I promise you that taking advantage of the meetings organized by these parents' associations are ideal places if you feel like meeting new people. You will naturally meet people who are like you, who think like you and together you will find activities that suit you and make you happy.

I remember that in Asia, sport in international schools had an extremely important place. As soon as the trial days were announced, parents rushed to get a place for their children. The long-term aim was for the children to be on the school team and represent the school across Asia. These inter-school competitions were an important highlight of the year. All the students of the school were invited to come and support their teams. These events were very well organized and it was a great pride for the parents and the school to send or receive their best athletes. Students were always accommodated in the foreign country in a family of the school hosting the competition. Usually, the students would stay in pairs. That's how we got two volleyball players from Singapore to stay at our house for a weekend.

Dan was originally from Singapore and David was British. The first day, after their first competitions, I remember picking them up from school. On the way, I understood from the conversation that Dan was turning 18 that same day. I could not let such an event go unnoticed and asked him what he would like for dinner. Not having any specific desire, I suggested that he try a food he had never tasted before. Delighted with the idea, we went with our guests and Constantin and Angelina to a Lebanese restaurant. My children were much younger than they were, but the dinner and the pictures we took are still a great memory. The bond was made and the whole weekend we went to watch them play. We were caught up in this wonderful atmosphere. Both my children still remember this weekend as a special moment of their school time in Manila!

Learning the language...

When I arrived in Mexico City, I had my Portuguese diploma in my pocket, but I didn't speak a word of Spanish... I had to learn a new language. Even though the two languages have similar Latin roots, I soon realized that if I didn't take Spanish classes, I would be speaking "Portognol" (a mix of Spanish and Portuguese) the whole time I was there. I quickly enrolled in university and every morning I went to take my classes with young students who were in Mexico City on an exchange program. I was 37 years old, the oldest in the class, but I enjoyed being there.

Unfortunately, the swine flu in 2009 interrupted all our programs. Life in Mexico City came to a halt, our company asked us to leave Mexico immediately and return to Switzerland for the summer. What a disaster! Mexico was my house, my home. I had my furniture there, the children were happy in their school. As a family we had to leave everything, our new friends, our new life. We were running away, leaving our dog behind once again and what if it had lasted longer than the summer?

Fortunately, that first pandemic was nothing like the COVID-19 pandemic; however, to see a capital city stop breathing, to not see anyone on the way to the airport, was a real shock. During COVID-19, when the world has been paralyzed for more than a year, I realize how lucky we were to have been able to return to Switzerland just for the summer and to have been able to resume our Mexican life in September; the swine flu had lasted for only a few months and was now just a bad memory.

When I returned in September, I continued my Spanish lessons at home with a private teacher. Even though I had acquired the necessary vocabulary to get by in everyday life, I loved this language so much that I wanted to take advantage of this opportunity to improve my grammar and more.

Each Latin American country has its own expressions and accents. When you speak Mexican, you speak Spanish with a certain accent and expressions that are unique to Mexico. Personally, I enjoyed learning all their expressions and trying to have an accent as close to theirs as possible and talking with my Mexican friends as if I were one of them! In fact, they always told me that it always made them laugh to hear a little Swiss girl talking like them.

We all have our own methods of learning. For me, I remember that when I lived in Indonesia, between 2003 and 2006, I learned a few Bahasa Indonesian vocabulary words every time I sat in the car. I had my little vocabulary cards and just like in school, I reviewed my words. Learning this language was necessary in Indonesia to communicate with the locals. The Indonesians often spoke only Bahasa Indonesian and the dialect of their village, so relying on their abilities to speak English was not an option.

In other countries, like here in the UAE, learning the local language is not a necessity. Nobody expects you to learn

Arabic. All government information is translated into English and the locals are proud to speak English to you. The UAE is a country that is 90% inhabited by expats. In the UAE, English is the language to learn.

By my few examples throughout this book, you can see that in each country, the priorities for integration are different. If in the Philippines it was for me to understand the Filipinos as people, in Jakarta, Brazil and Mexico, it was really to learn the language.

In all countries, my husband, because of his work and his daily mixing with the locals, like me, also had to learn the language of each country.

This effort has also allowed us to mix with a wider and more varied circle of people and our family was regularly invited to join family lunches and weekends at Mexican homes. These experiences gave us the opportunity to experience the country at a deeper level.

In addition to communions and weddings, we were invited to private bullfights, private artists' exhibitions, concerts.... a series of events that allowed us to discover the country from a different angle.

A first...

One of my most memorable and original experiences in Mexico was bullfighting with my friend Moni.

It is in their family *hacienda* that Moni and all her family often meet on weekends. Grandparents, brothers, sisters, cousins, all come together to experience the happiness of the countryside and the family. On their land they raise bulls, a family tradition that leads each generation to bullfight on foot or even on horseback. This is a family passion that they also like to share with their friends. Once, Alex, Angelina, Constantin and I had the chance to join their traditional Mexican family weekend.

After a wonderful country lunch, we were invited to gather around their arena. The *ganaderos* started to bring out some young bulls so that everyone could make some passes with these young but powerful animals. At first, I was impressed and was content to watch while the experimenters demonstrated, but then the urge to try for myself got stronger, and when Moni offered, Alex and I could not resist. It was a unique opportunity. The atmosphere was of course very friendly and I was confident with Moni in the arena. Moni taught me the basic moves, the little bull was set loose and although I was scared at first, I soon found it exhilarating! I remember this weekend as a great moment of sharing, friendship and happiness!

Regardless of the country, these types of life experiences, so close to the native, have occurred because local people appreciate our interest in their culture.

The opportunity to discover more places, cultures and foods...

When you are based in a certain city in a country, it is like living in a hub for the next few years. You just want to spread out to the whole country, meet the locals, exchange ideas, share a bit of their daily life and enjoy all that the country has to offer. Whether it's in the country itself or in neighboring countries, it's a unique opportunity to visit places that are often far from our home country. By being closer geographically, we can go back several times and enjoy it for longer. I must admit that the arrival of the children has never limited our travels. We quickly got them used to our pace, which always made them easy, flexible and happy to be part of all our trips.

When I look back on my life, I realize that every day I had the chance to meet at least one new person, my eyes saw something new, tasted a different taste, breathed a new smell, discovered a new place, learned something new about my host country or witnessed a new scene of life. While keeping my values, this diversity has really enriched me and naturally influenced my habits. Today for example, our at-home food is much more varied, our taste has developed and if before my long expatriate adventure, I could not eat spice, today I am used to it. Little by little, I integrate in my daily life what I prefer in each culture and honestly, I do not make the distinction anymore. I have mixed my traditions, my habits, with those I met on the way and it is often others who point this out to me. We created our own culture, our own identity, and this is how we became "citizens of the world."

Connections...

Even today, almost 10 years later, not a day goes by that I do not have a message exchange on social networks with my friends from around the world.

For me as an expat, social networks are a gold mine. A daily connection with my past, with the people who made my life, my memories. Lately I've been having fun going through my private Facebook and Instagram accounts to see if I could remember every single one of my friends. Not only did I remember every single one of them, but even more amazingly, I can visualize a memory for each person that we will always have in common.

Social networks are also such an easy way to stay in touch and connect two people who might want to meet. How often can a simple message to a friend help another friend find an answer to a question I can't help them with?

I have always loved to maintain and seek this connection and bond with others. This is probably why I am so committed to my career as a coach. This job fits so well with my aspirations. Thanks to coaching, and in coaching expatriates, I am able to recapture the emotions I felt during my expatriation experiences. Coaching allows me to stay in touch with this world, this diversity, this mix of differences and similarities. To go and meet people who live even outside the country where I live.

Through video conferencing (digital communication apps), I connect with individuals based all over the world. Whether in India, Asia, the Americas or Europe, we can now have a session as if we were in the same city. If before COVID-19 this means of communication was an obstacle for some, today it is becoming more and more natural and easy for most people, and I think it always has been in the expat world, a world in which communication despite any geographical barriers is quickly becoming a priority.

The world today is more connected than ever and if physically we are still far away, we are really lucky to be able to communicate easily with our relatives, our coaches and clients!

Reflections...

To help identify what experiences you are looking for in the expatriation life, I invite you to reflect on these questions:

- What experiences are you looking for in your life?

- What are your priorities for yourself?

- What makes you accept a new situation?

CHAPTER

EIGHT

You can create your home anywhere

Just settling in...

While arriving in a new country can be exciting, it can also be stressful.

It often takes a few weeks to get administratively settled in a city. The bureaucracy is often much slower than one would like. Again, you have to remember that there are things that you can control and those things that you have to put up with. You can often lose patience at the beginning of an expatriation.

However, I would like to share some things you can do that will help you to integrate more quickly. For example, registering at your embassy allows you to feel safe and to be informed of all the necessary information. We belong to a community, and we know that in case of any problems, our embassy will do what is necessary to inform us of the procedure, or even repatriate us or inform our family in our country of origin. The receptions organized by the embassy are also a way to meet other expats and locals who live in the country.

Today, having a telephone and a local telephone number is much easier than it had been in the past. This is a means that allows family members to stay in constant contact. Even if we depend a lot on our phone, it is still a way to stay connected and reassure each other, and it allows us to feel secure and independent.

I remember my first outing in the city in the Philippines. Excited to discover Manila and sure of myself, I left home feeling confident, but I quickly realized that I was in an environment that I didn't know yet, I had to familiarize myself with it. Especially in this time of transition, I found myself overwhelmed with anxiety and the desire to be with my family.

When we arrived in the Philippines, it was the time of the monsoons. I had been warned that the rains could be torrential but I did not expect to what extent. We had just arrived, we were staying in a hotel, the children had started school and were taking the school bus.

That morning, I left the hotel in a light rain to go with the driver of the office to the embassy. It was the day before a long weekend; we had planned to travel and I needed our passports. The embassy was a few kilometers away as the crow flew but I soon found myself in the middle of heavy rain and the water was beginning to rise to the level of the car doors. In Manila, there are no gutters, so the water does not drain away easily so as soon as it rains, the city floods very quickly. By experience (because in Indonesia it's exactly the same) I know that if you are caught in these floods, you can spend many hours stuck there without being able to move.

As a precaution and not being familiar with the city or the area yet, I quickly asked the driver to take me back to the hotel. Suddenly I felt anxious and so alone. My children were on one side of the city, my husband on the other side and I was in this car, in the middle of a totally foreign environment with the driver, a person I hardly knew. However, the locals did not seem to share in my panic – I still remember the image of those Filipinos so calmly sweeping the water that came to their door. These torrential rains seemed to be a very familiar situation for them.

When I arrived in my hotel room on the eighth floor, I was amazed by the spectacle I had under my windows, but the wait for the return of my children seemed eternal. They were to arrive with the school bus. The school assistant in the bus regularly informed us by message of the bus's progress, until they finally got home, and I hugged them in relief. I admit that my reaction seems exaggerated, but I promise you that in times of transition, we are all much more sensitive and emotional.

Home sweet home...

I have found that there are always a few words in each language that I respond to and connect with. In Spanish, the word "*hogar*" (meaning "home") is one that I find very powerful. To me, this word represents refuge, unity, connection and harmony, describing what I feel is my responsibility: to provide my husband and children with a home, a warm place, a real comfort.

I have always taken to heart the decoration of our home and the importance of feeling good in it – something that my mother probably passed on to me, as I remember always living in cozy and nicely-decorated environments.

Alex and I moved from Switzerland to Africa with a few personal items: our books, photo albums, clothes, part of our tableware, CDs but no furniture. We took with us the souvenirs that would best connect us to our past and we used them as a way to feel at home, by creating a familiar environment.

Normally we would have taken our furniture but in West Africa there is a wind called the harmattan: a dry wind that dries the wood and makes the furniture crack. We chose to leave our most precious belongings in a storage facility in Switzerland, meaning we had to find a new way to bring "home" into our house. Our house in Africa was spacious, and the few pieces of furniture sold on the roadside inspired me very little. I quickly took ideas from various magazines and tried to have my designs copied or more often than not, my drawings. It was a very fun experience, but the result was rarely perfect.

As I mentioned before, while each company has its own conditions, I know that some expatriates have to leave without furniture and are compensated to buy what they need locally. Before leaving, I think it's important to find out what the conditions are and what you can find in the host country. For some people this is a more difficult concept than for others, not to mention that in some countries it is difficult to find furniture easily and even more so at reasonable prices. While Ikea is unfortunately not present in all countries, in Brazil, for example, furniture was also extremely expensive. I remember a television costing the price of 12'000 USD on sale – outrageous but true!

I remember often meeting families who could not furnish their home for months and this was undoubtedly an obstacle to settling and affected the wellbeing of a family in a new country.

Our furniture reflects our lives...

In each country we also collected some pieces that are really part of our history. I can describe the exact place where we bought every piece; the price negotiation, the environment and the smells (I am very sensitive to smells!). We have, for example, a beautiful elephant at home sculpted out of one piece of wood. I spotted it in Cotonou in a tourist souvenir market where I used to go every time I had guests visiting us. At first, the price was too high and each time I returned to the market, I negotiated further, and eventually got the price I wanted. In Africa, as in many countries, you never pay the first price, it is the culture to negotiate: at that time, in any case, the sellers really played the game.

This elephant really caught my attention. At first, I bargained for fun, but the more I went back, the more I wanted to take it home. I set myself a maximum price but I must admit that after a few months, I ended up being afraid that for a few CFA francs (the local currency) I would miss out on the purchase, so I broke down and brought back my elephant, which still stands in my living room today.

We were also lucky enough to move from Africa to Indonesia: a furniture paradise at a time when Indonesian furniture was also very in vogue. I greatly enjoyed the process of shopping for these pieces, and was able to furnish my house completely. Today, some pieces are a bit outdated, but we still keep and use the same furniture because not only is it still beautiful, but above all they are our history. Our children were born and raised in this environment and despite the fact that everything around them changes regularly, they are happy to find in each country a home environment that is familiar to them. As well as mementos for me and my husband, these pieces are markers for our children.

When people come to our house, they are always amazed at how well our house reflects our life as global nomads. Over the years we have naturally accumulated furniture, souvenirs, objects and paintings. Many of our artworks are paintings that I have done myself.

My philosophy has always been to move into a house as if we were going to stay there for life. If the environment changes, very quickly the interior follows and resembles the previous home.

To feel homely and comfortable can take more time than one would think. In this transitional phase, I also think of the children for whom landmarks are important. I have always enjoyed watching my children's excitement at picking out their room, dreaming of how they would arrange it, organize it and decorate it to recreate their world. I do not know if it's specific to my children or to all expat children, but I notice that Constantin and Angelina spend a lot of time in their room; it's really their nest. Their room is also very organized: every object has its place, and every place has its object. Perhaps they are like me, they like to have their own things around them, things that they can rely on to be there anywhere they go. For them, their rooms are places of refuge where they can create stability and comfort.

For them, as for us, decorating our home is important for our balance. We are all sensitive to our environment, we like to familiarize ourselves with it to feel comfortable and safe.

I have always liked to keep a lot of photos and artworks in our home, reminding us of all of our life memories and keeping our family present: grandparents, godparents, cousins and close friends. It's a way for us to link, to connect all these episodes of life, that we live in one unique expatriate life.

Each member of the family has its way to find its place...

We know that moving house or country has an extremely strong emotional impact on people. There are four of us in the family and each of us experiences this change very differently. I feel that this is a time when you really have to let the individual experience this moment at his or her own pace so that, little by little, he or she can find himself or herself, and be in agreement and at peace with himself or herself. In the end, each person, in turn, will find their place. Do not forget, that if in the life of an expatriate you need to have patience, in this transitional phase, it is even more important.

Moving to a new city also means getting used to it: discovering your neighborhood, knowing where to go to find a particular product. You start to have a certain sense of orientation in the city, your reactions become more automatic, you know the way to the school or to your husband's office, you recognize people because you see them regularly. Or, like us, we had one or two restaurants in each country that became almost like our canteens because we ate there so regularly.

When the announcement of a move is made, my husband, an epicurean, extrovert, bon vivant and always positive, will immediately start his research on the internet. He will explore things to do, places to visit, restaurants to try, trips to go on. In relation to our lifestyle, he will even determine which neighborhood we should live in, he may have already spotted the house we are going to live in on google map!

His enthusiastic attitude is a big part of the success of our expat life and our life in general. Thanks to his constant good humor, generosity of heart, empathy and dynamism, we are constantly living in a positive energy. His energy is also extremely communicative and allows us all to keep on moving despite any struggles that we may face, and to always see the positive side of situations.

As I mentioned earlier, Alex is also very family-oriented. This is one of the strong pillars of our family's success. Alex manages his professional life in such a way that he is always there when one of us needs him. For me, his wife, I have always felt that I was his priority; that I was accompanied and supported. For our children, even though their father often lived away from them during the week, when he was present, he was really there for them.

My daughter, Angelina, is still young and is very much part of a family dynamic. She is always happy when she is with her brother and her parents. For her, the most important thing is to understand the sequence of events and the planning behind them. She doesn't like to be surprised or unaware of what's going to happen. Angelina is a very organized girl – she is independent and has always asked a lot of questions. It's her way of reassuring herself. We have always taken care to listen to her and answer her questions so that the answer gives her the comfort she needs.

Very sociable, Angelina has always had few friends but strong relationships. She has grown up with social media and while keeping in touch with old friends used to be a challenge in the past, for young people of her generation it is now much easier to keep in touch over time. It still takes effort, but it has undoubtedly become much more accessible. Angelina is in regular contact with her friends in Mexico, the Philippines, Europe and around the world.

Special bond...

Being very attached to Mexico, we went back on holiday to see our friends there. We felt like we had never left, we were picking up the story exactly where we left off.

While in Mexico, most of Angelina's friends were Mexican and would never live abroad, in the Philippines and Dubai, her friends are also mostly expatriates like her. In turn, families move away and scatter around the world. All the children also see their friends come and go.

This summer, while we were on holiday in Italy, Angelina told us that she had spotted a friend on one of her apps who was in the same town. It took them a few minutes to exchange two or three messages, set up a time and spend a few totally unexpected hours together. This story shows how much technological progress will help us expats feel more connected to our world, to our friends, to our loved ones.

Recreating a family in its new environment...

As parents, we also have to play a role model, an inspirational role. Creating a home also means developing a life outside of the family, developing a social life and seeking to surround oneself with people who can become true friends, to share moments of leisure, happiness and trust. People that we look forward to meeting on a regular basis. It is a way of demonstrating to our kids that wherever you settle, you can be happy and create tight relationships with a circle with whom you can share your time, your sports, your ideas, your interests.

We invest in relationships: we host at home, we are invited between parents or with the whole family to other people's homes, we organize activities or even trips. With time, young and old, we create memories and bonding that will be an integral part of our adventure in these countries.

The reality of expat life is that some friendships end naturally when we leave the country, or we choose to maintain them and make the effort to make them survive time and distance. However, I like to note that we have remained very close to certain families that we enjoy meeting up with on holiday even though we are now living different adventures in different countries. It is not impossible to keep these relationships alive and they are integral to keeping a familiar support network for yourself and your children.

Keeping relationships alive...

If you are geographically far from your family and friends, they are often the ones who are happy to come and see you and share what you are experiencing abroad. The time you spend together, even if it is less frequent, becomes in any case more intense and certainly very qualitative, a privileged opportunity to strengthen the bonds between children and family. Our grandparents like to come once a year to spend a few weeks with us. For them it's really a special time to spend quality time with their grandchildren.

Having visitors is also an opportunity to share our world, our life, what we do and what we know. It feels great! Our guests participate in our daily life, they can see us live, are included and can experience a taste of our life for a while. For them this is an opportunity to feel, to understand our choice, to see us in our environment when they are far away. There is time to discuss, to exchange. We return to this model, this example, to realize how important it is for children to observe how possible and important it is to keep a link with our roots, with our culture, with our past.

Inversely, when we have a holiday, we travel and meet our families and friends. Most of the time we go back to Austria or Switzerland, but we have also seen friends we met during a posting in their new destinations.

I would like to take this opportunity to thank my sister-in-law, her husband and their five children, who every summer receive us with open arms for several weeks. Thanks to them, we have always had a wonderful time and the cousins have really developed strong relationships. A bond for the future.

Maintaining the culture...

When I am alone with my children, I have always made it a point to speak French, my mother tongue. Even if they answer me in another language, I like to paraphrase in French what they say and continue the discussion in French. Constantin has always liked to communicate with me in French, for him it was a bit like having a secret language.

In addition to the language, we live in a European way at home. I have never had a particular interest in cooking, so when I hire a helper, I insist that she knows how to cook, especially European cuisine. This is a priority for me, so I prefer to take my time and hire the person who meets my needs. If it seems demanding and complicated, with a bit of patience and through the rich expat networks, one can find some gems. Today Julie successfully cooks all the dishes of my childhood. Either she learned to cook from cookbooks translated into English, or my mother spent time in the kitchen and showed her some recipes. As a tradition, for every birthday, Julie learned to bake an Austrian cake, a special recipe that came from Alex's family. This cake was called an *Oblatten*. Unfortunately, it was not us who stopped the tradition, but the biscuit suppliers... the production is stopped for the moment... what a pity!

Reflections...

To help identify what makes your environment safe for you I invite you to reflect on these questions:

- What are the best conditions you can put in place for you and your family to facilitate change?

- What elements make your home a comfortable and safe place for your family?

- What values and traditions are important to you? How could you preserve and perpetuate them to be closer to your culture?

CHAPTER

NINE

You will always meet friends that feel like family

What if you trust in the universe...

Just before leaving for Indonesia, by chance I met my friend Cristobel in Geneva. This meeting completely changed my experience of Jakarta. In the space of one dinner in Geneva, my life came together. All the stars aligned. Cristobel put me in touch with Frederique, a friend of hers who was about to leave Jakarta.

In addition to all the basic information I needed, Frederique had just enough time to recommend and introduce me to her household staff who had not only worked for her, but also for her in-laws, who were themselves expatriates 20 years earlier in Jakarta. To be able to welcome into our new life, into our house, staff who were recommended to us is for me a great opportunity. It was a mutual trust that was established from the beginning.

Because of the movement that takes place between the departures and arrivals of expatriates, there are always ways to get good staff recommended by a family that is leaving the country. These staff are already familiar with working for foreigners and therefore often respond better to our needs/requests.

Frederique moved from Jakarta to Singapore, and as you already know, I gave birth to Constantin in Singapore. Frederique was generously welcoming me at her place whenever I went for my check-ups in Singapore. Each month I was lucky enough to meet up with my friend and enjoy Singapore in the best possible conditions. Part of the reason why Constantin is called that name is because Frederique's youngest son was called Constantin. Besides the fact that Alex and I liked the name very much, I wanted to thank my friend and express my gratitude for everything she had done for me those last months.

Dubai...

As you may have noticed, I do not talk much about our expatriation to Dubai because it is an experience that for me and my family is very different from others. Dubai is our sixth expatriation and I must admit that the practical challenges of moving to other countries have not been the same in Dubai. The experiences we have accumulated with all our previous transitions have prepared us well on the one hand and on the other hand, Dubai being 90% populated by expatriates, all the administrations are well-organized so that we as foreigners, can settle in easily and quickly.

However, I fully understand and respect that Dubai can also be a city where it is difficult to integrate administratively and socially when you do not know anyone on arrival. It is true that unlike a country where the daily life of the expatriate is a real challenge and therefore the expatriate community is very close and supportive, in Dubai, life being easier, more organized, I am personally less aware of the associations that help with integration in the country.

The Dubai experience started differently from other expatriations because I was going to live the "split family" experience. Alex would be in Pakistan during the week and would come back home at weekends. I must admit that my coaching sessions with Maud had prepared me well and this new expatriation experience, although difficult at times, finally went extremely well. I had arrived in Dubai emotionally ready and had also decided to take online courses, both in interior design and life coaching. The children found their rhythm very quickly.

Constantin was very involved in his passion for go-karting and Angelina was also very sporty and enjoyed her gym classes. Alex always came home on the weekend. However, every evening, in order to have a little family time, we would put the iPad on the dining room table so that Alex could share our dinner and our daily stories. It was a nice way to keep him up-to-date with what the kids were going through at school and for their dad to tell us what he was experiencing away from us. In this way, we never really felt separated, it was our way of getting together for our family dinner.

I soon discovered that my split family situation was extremely common here in Dubai. Many families are stationed in Dubai, but the partners work for weeks or even months in other surrounding countries.

I would also like to take a moment to acknowledge and share my sympathies with all the families who during COVID-19 were separated for months because the borders were closed overnight.

Plug and play...

On a social level, as an adult, Dubai did not require much effort. We had a unique chance, which in my opinion is extremely rare in expatriation, in that we found our childhood friends here. Friends with whom our first memories go back even further than primary school.

Caroline, my bridesmaid and precious friend since school, was above all the best ambassador of Dubai, having lived in and loved the city for over 10 years. While Caroline was my first connection to Dubai, she was my main confidante when I was still posted in Manila and couldn't reveal our transfer plans to my entourage. Thanks to her enthusiasm, recommendations and connections, I was able to begin to visualize my future life from a distance and to actively make plans.

Our arrival in Dubai was unique and extraordinary: in a holiday destination, reconnecting with past friendships, and introducing our own children was a blessing for our family. For our children, this expatriation was also very different. They soon felt welcomed and integrated into groups of which they immediately felt a part. The arrival in Dubai was therefore very smooth for them too. We have found families in Dubai with whom our friendships go back so far that our children are even the fourth generation to be friends!

The chances are that Dubai will be our last expatriation and I'm glad that our postings happened in that order. If I had started here, I would probably have been surprised or even discouraged by the greater effort that other cities require to integrate.

Time to go out of your comfort zone...

With the exception of Dubai, I had never arrived in an expatriation post where I found a person I knew personally. Of course, Alex was arriving in a more familiar environment, as he was joining work colleagues. In most countries, Alex would have work colleagues whose families were also living in the country. In these cases, it was easy for me to make contact with their wives, meet and ask the first practical questions that would allow me to get out of my nest. With some families we had affinities and even got together on weekends. However, I think it is easily understandable that partners also like to separate their professional and private lives and at weekends they also want to change their environment and talk about something other than their work.

So, I had to get out of my house very quickly and start to network!

Here I would also like to reassure you that any woman who has lived abroad is aware of how difficult it can be to get out of your comfort zone and reach out to others. Each of us in our own way has had our down moments and preferred to find an excuse to avoid going to a cafe gathering or a parents' meeting... it's normal and it is not unusual to feel like that. Everyone has their own rhythm, and you will know when it is the right time. However, there may be times when it is helpful to be bold! The reality is that no one will look for you! You need to go out there. The first effort should be yours, that's the secret! When you meet your first friend, expatriation takes on a whole new dimension. You will eventually surround yourself with the right people, people who will bring out the best in you!

If we accept that friendship is based on shared passions, common interests or similar tastes, then we can start by choosing activities and opportunities that will allow us to meet people we can relate to.

Often the groups are organized by common languages or by country. But do not let this first discovery overwhelm you, because as soon as you have something in common with these groups, you will be welcomed with open arms. Many of these associations are non-political and run by volunteers who are concerned with the wellbeing of all expatriates, regardless of nationality.

Arriving in Manila, I joined the Latinas group, simply because I had lived in Mexico for five years. I was attached to this culture and I wanted to continue my South American experience. My Swiss passport did not predestine me to be part of this group, but given my background and my affinity for their culture, these women opened their hearts to me!

Young (or not so young) first time expatriates can often be impressed by such gatherings of women in expat groups. I have been overwhelmed by the energy, welcome and kindness expressed by older women in the expat community and would encourage you not to make age a barrier and to stay curious and explore these relationships. You may not be intimidated by preconceived opinions!

There are many ways to meet people...

Often before you leave for your new posting, you can join expat groups on social media and ask all the questions you have about the place and modes of life there. These first virtual contacts can also inform you about local associations and put you in contact with people who can help you find the answers you are looking for. In the beginning, a lot of good advice is passed on by word of mouth. Within these newcomer groups, there are often sub-groups such as young mothers' groups, activity groups, language groups, sports groups and more.

I remember that in Indonesia and the Philippines, the American women organized extraordinary bazaars that offered the local artisans and the expatriate women to present their products and the opportunity to discover the local products and to find out what was available in that country. These bazaars were always very popular and a great way to meet expatriate women in an expatriate atmosphere.

I would also like to highlight that it is the expatriate women themselves who run these groups and when they leave the country, another expatriate will take on the role. Joining these groups, of very active and committed women, is also a way to integrate into your host country and expatriate community. I met many women who were seeking these responsibilities and joining these event groups in all the countries where they were expatriates.

Meeting other mothers at school...

Having small children, school was the ideal place to meet other mothers easily.

I will never forget my arrival at Miraflores, the local Mexican school. This was the school that Constantin would attend first, and where Angelina would join him a few years later. Constantin arrived from Brazil speaking fluent Portuguese, French and a few words of English but not a word of Spanish. He was five years old.

From the beginning, the mothers welcomed us warmly and very quickly Constantin had some playdates. I cannot say enough about how friendly and welcoming Mexicans are. Whenever I brought or picked up my son, I was invited to stay and share a tequila... or a cup of tea. At first, I did not speak Spanish either and they made a real effort to speak English to me. I soon took my Spanish lessons; I was so excited to speak that I could not miss an opportunity to practice with them. I must admit that I was very lucky to have met women who were curious, empathic and who did everything to make me love their country and their people.

I met Elisa in Mexico. She had twins the same age as my son and a little girl the same age as Angelina. A strong friendship developed between us and between the children. To this day, Angelina communicates regularly with her friend. Angelina talks about her as a friend who always puts her in a good mood, a loyal and loving friend. Despite their young age when they met and then separated, they are still very close today. More importantly, they both took a long time to be able to befriend a new friend in such a strong way.

Elisa came to me because of my adventurous attitude. She always found it quite unbelievable that I regularly got into my car and went off to explore Mexico City on my own. Even though I learned Spanish quickly, she found my attitude courageous knowing that Mexico City is a very dangerous megalopolis.

I would make sure to dress simply and keep my wits about me as I ventured to all parts of the city to discover its richness. For me those adventures were a kind of magic and made me so happy. As I had done in every previous country, I was enjoying every bit of Mexico and the life it was offering us. My time in the country was limited, so I took every opportunity to discover it. I regularly discovered new restaurants, shops, museums, and I remember that my local friends often asked me for my addresses and also went to discover places in their country that they did not know yet.

Living in Mexico and developing friendships with Mexican women like Elisa has taught me a lot about the meaning of values in Mexico. The sense of family, friends, mutual aid and trust are fundamental values in Mexico, values that are also very dear to me. I liked knowing that my children were growing up with these same ideals. Mexico gave me a real kick-start in my life and our time in this country helped me to grow and gain confidence in what I wanted from life for myself and for my children.

My dear friend Moni has been a real mentor for me during these five years in Mexico. Moni and I used to talk a lot. I learned a lot from her experience and she learned a lot from mine. I watched her raise her five children (older than mine). It was a real life lesson. I saw how genuine she was, how much love and energy she put into supporting her children in their passions, in their sports and in their studies. Her children were flourishing and each one of them was at their best in their own discipline. There was a lot of work, organization and energy behind the scenes of their success. Moni managed to be there for each child individually while never forgetting herself, her husband or her friends. Her state of mind, strength and positive energy has inspired me a lot. A gift to me, this strong friendship has enriched me enormously and given me a boost in life!

The richness of expatriation is that you too are a new source of energy and curiosity. In a new relationship, you are not the only one to receive, you also have a lot to offer. Your cultural differences, your background and experiences are also of interest to your friends, who are also happy to meet someone who has a new energy and a different way of looking at things.

Friendship is generous, based on trust and respect...

Through our new friendships, we also learn a lot about the diversity of cultures and how each of us reacts differently to situations.

Sometimes surprised, often fascinated, I was always curious to understand how the culture of the country I was living in impacted on people's ideas, especially those of my friends.

I remember long conversations with my friends in which we discovered how each of us had different ways of thinking. I would listen to them and realize that ultimately their ideas, like mine, were shaped by our childhood experiences, including the cultural environment we grew up with, and the challenges we faced. Our different perspectives on life made our discussions engaging. They were also very respectful, never judgmental and above all very constructive.

In our sharing aloud, we would become aware of how our own ideas impacted our adult lives, affecting our perceptions, our limits and possibilities. Our assumptions could also be obstacles to what we could achieve and the success we could have.

Our different cultural backgrounds were a source of stimulating exchanges that often gave us the opportunity to open up to new views and possibilities. For my friends, as for me, it was an opportunity to create room for new ambitions, to set new life goals, to grow and take our lives to the next level!

Keep in touch!

If there is one thing my family and I have really experienced during these 25 years of expatriation, it has been an evolution and transformation of communication, both in form and in substance!

When we arrived in Africa, we did not send letters by post. This was a time when emails were becoming accessible, although we still often wrote our emails in the form of a letter. It was also the time of SMS. It was so easy to leave a quick message for anyone to give them any updates or news. Thanks to this efficient communication, we always felt close to our family and friends.

Before social media, in the first years of my expatriation, I enjoyed making newsletters every year in January, in the format of small texts and photos. I sent the summary of our adventures of the year. For many expat families, newsletters had replaced our greeting cards. It was a very personal and wonderful way to keep in touch with our families, old friends and new friends, those we had met during our first expatriations. I can remember that these newsletters had a strong impact on our relatives, they loved to reply, loved to see pictures of what we were experiencing and to see the children growing up. These newsletters also gave the opportunity to revive relationships that otherwise may have faded.

I also understand that some people do not like social media and therefore do not use it. In cases like this, I try to remember the birthdays of these friends and send them a little message. Time goes by very quickly, but I make the effort to check in each year.

Every friendship is as unique as it is precious. Life circumstances make some friendships last longer than others but they all have a special place in my journey. Nevertheless, I have tried to remind myself not to feel guilty about letting a friendship fade away.

You are not the only one responsible for maintaining a friendship: remember that the person also has the means to contact you. Regardless, it is natural for friendships to drift away and come back together, or stay permanently apart – there is no right or wrong formula for friendship, and remembering the positive moments is often the best thing we can do.

Live in the moment, enjoy yourself, make the effort to hold onto those who are dear to you, and continue to trust that whatever comes next, you can handle it!

All ages are the right age for a new adventure...

I would like to share with you the story of my friend Christina for whom expatriation came later in life. Her experience shows how life is a succession of surprises and expatriation is an opportunity that can present itself at any time!

Christina is sharing her story...

"That's it! We're leaving..." I turn the key to the door and I feel a twinge of sadness, a few tears in the corner of my eye... one does not leave one's city and one's home, without any qualms; one does not move towards a new life, without apprehension.

Besides a major move in my twenties, my experience of expatriation had the particularity to intervene at the "third age" not to say "at an advanced age," after having spent my whole life in the same city and practically in the same neighborhood.

It is rather rare to leave your life and habits at an age where usually one wishes or is supposed to have a good rest, to live without (too) many constraints, while organizing enough activities to give rhythm to our days and not to find oneself in front of "a blank page."

My husband had a working project abroad, but in order not to impose his decision on me, separating me from my family, he had kindly proposed to arrange our life with a *modus vivendi*, allowing us to see each other regularly. This option was a "non-option" for me.

Once the decision to leave was made, I had to get down to the work, which I personally found quite difficult, that of sorting things out. Whether you are moving (taking your home with you) or moving in a "lighter" sense, you have to sort, tidy, choose among the objects accumulated over a lifetime. As painful as this experience can be, it was finally very rich and beneficial; but I am not going to advocate Marie Kondo's art of tidying up here.

I am not going to enumerate here the practical advice to prepare your expatriation. However, if I had to summarize, to facilitate your integration, you can prepare yourself in advance, in order to "control" the situation as much as possible, so that it seems less frightening. Despite this, it is very likely that only little will be as we planned or expected.

Your attitude will therefore be decisive. You have two choices: either you get frustrated or angry, and you will be unhappy; or you find the good side, you laugh about it, adapt and put all the chances on your side, to move forward.

The way you see the glass as half empty or half full will only depend on you, on your ability to look and find (yes, you have to be a little proactive!) the positive aspect to a given situation.

In a more practical way, and regarding my personal experience, I would say that "curiosity" in its broadest sense, is my engine at 100%. Curiosity is to open wide your eyes and your ears, to open up your soul and your heart.

Talking to people, visiting places, finding new activities, signing up for language courses or discovering the local culture, doing a (new) sport, walking in the city, discovering local artists and craftsmen, volunteering, observing, traveling, you name it ... the possibilities to get off the beaten track to be closer to this new life are endless and so exciting.

The resulting satisfactions have been an almost mathematical equation of my investment and my "curiosity."

When you understand that you are the only one you can count on and that you are in the driver's seat, it gives you a feeling of power and strength, and as a consequence, satisfaction and self-esteem.

I couldn't be more enthusiastic about my experience, even if the timing seemed, at first glance, counterintuitive, anachronistic. "Come on, you don't go abroad at retirement age!"

I encourage you to reconsider your eventual prejudices and take courage (and your life in hand) to live this adventure. You will be surprised to realize how this "third age" turns out to be a fulfilling "new" age, energetic, stimulating, rewarding and keeping us so young at heart.

Reflections...

To help you identify what will help you rebuild your social environment, I invite you to think about these questions:

- What is important for you to reconnect with if/when you move abroad?

- What might hold you back from forming new friendships?

- What has made your relationships successful to date?

CHAPTER

TEN

Raising TCK, Third Culture Kids

Understanding the concept of a third culture child is important to me because it can answer important questions about identity, belonging and many other issues. In my opinion, being clearer on this topic may also strengthen and consolidate your relationship with your children, even if you have not experienced being a child of a third culture.

Ruth Hill Useem (1915 – 2003) was an American sociologist and anthropologist who introduced the concept of Third Culture Kid (TCK) to describe children who spent part of their developmental years in a foreign culture due to their parents working abroad. Her work was the first to identify common themes among various TCK's that may affect them throughout their lives. Third Culture Kids include military brats, missionary kids, diplomatic kids, and business kids. Many books have been written on Third Culture Kids and "Global Nomads" based on the concept originally proposed and defined by Useem.

For most parents, our children are the most precious thing in the world and we want the best for them. The question is, how do we determine what is actually best for each individual?

Alex and I have always wanted to share with our children the life that inspires us and makes us happy. The life that we want to evolve in, that makes us curious, that allows our children to grow up with us, filled with love and the emotional richness we can offer them.

As parents, we have never felt worried about raising our children in countries far from our home countries. We have always seen expatriation, and especially expatriation as we have been fortunate enough to experience it, as an extraordinary opportunity for our children to learn and grow.

Our children are true "global nomads." I have the impression that today, in the era of globalization, it is a real advantage for children to acquire, from a very young age, cross-cultural competencies learned from their own priceless and unique experiences. Constantin and Angelina had the chance to learn different languages and meet people from all cultures, nationalities and backgrounds and to find connections and common grounds more quickly.

As I write this, we are still in the middle of the COVID-19 pandemic. It's been over 12 months since our lives have changed. Watching my children during this time, I can see how resilient and flexible they are. Very quickly they adapted to the new rules, to their new way of learning and living. Like all of us, they miss their old life, but little by little they change their habits to make the best of what they have.

Sometimes I dare to wonder if our expatriate children, who have known change since birth, have been better equipped than other children to deal with change. Perhaps they have had an advantage in the tumultuous changes and ordeals that we are currently going through?

From the moment Angelina was born (three years after Constantin) I was immediately aware that I had two totally different individuals with me. If I were to raise them with the values I believe in, my way of communicating and my expectations are totally different with each of them, because these two children are very different from each other.

This is probably why coaching conversations resonate with me so much – I probably had a subconscious need to think about how I would interact with each of them by really seeing them as a whole person.

I was lucky enough to be able to be very present and to spend a lot of time with them when they were young and particularly in need of it. I am ever proud of the bond, the connection and the closeness Alex and I have created with our children.

I have always enjoyed listening to them, asking them questions and really understanding their likes and dislikes. Learning what made them feel good, or what was fun and fulfilling for them. I feel that these discussions have empowered them to be active in their decisions and in their life.

I would like to make a point here, to observe how much my educational approach towards my children was ultimately based on coaching. In coaching, we believe that a client becomes totally independent from his coach when he manages to solve his problems alone with a way of thinking that allows him to create his own strategy to reach the goal he has set. Today I observe that my children are becoming more and more responsible, independent and self-confident, following this same pattern.

As much as I can share my own experience on this subject, I believe that the best feedback can only come from a TCK herself, who can share with us her personal experience, feelings and advice on this global nomad life.

Imogen's story...

In this chapter I would like to give a voice to Imogen, an 18-year-old TCK. Through her answers to my questions, we can have a better understanding of what these children can feel and how they react to the reality of expatriate life.

Where is home for you and what makes you feel that way?

I was born in Hong Kong, and lived there until I was five. Much of my family still lives there now. We also had many family friends that stayed there for a long time, a few of whom we are still connected to. My family then moved to Beijing and I lived there until I was 13, going to the same school the whole time. At 13 (in 2016), I decided that I wanted to go to boarding school in the UK, and moved away while my family stayed in Beijing. Two years later, while I was in my second year at boarding school, my family packed up and moved to Dubai, where they are still living. I am now 18 and in my last year at boarding school, planning to go to university in the UK.

When I first moved to the UK, people asked me "where is home for you?", and I said "China." At that time, my family, my friends, and my life was in Beijing. I quickly realized that the people I was surrounded by had had very different experiences to me: they had lived in the same house in the same place all their lives. They had gone to local schools, and had friends in their hometown. They saw their grandparents every Sunday for lunch, and had family reunions at Christmas. They knew exactly where their home was. At the time, so did I – and then we moved.

When we moved to Dubai, I left behind a whole life, never getting a chance to say goodbye. My friends from Beijing have since moved on, in the expatriate way, to various corners of the world, and we all acknowledged that we might not see each other ever again. For two years, I felt completely lost; home was a completely foreign concept to me. I barely ever came back to Dubai, and I had no friends there. Dubai did not feel like home at all.

So, I thought maybe my home could be at school, where I spent most of my time. However, at school I never had a safe space that could be mine alone; nothing belonged to me. I despaired over this for a while, and I began to dread the question "where is home for you?" because I could not hide my emotion when I answered that I did not know.

Now, I am preparing to leave boarding school after five years. I will be leaving behind a campus that has been the only constant in my life for a while now, along with my friends who have made it feel so welcoming. This is terrifying, and I would be lying if I said that I was ready. Constant change and not knowing where home is has made me cling to bits of familiarity – a scrap of paper from my boyfriend, a friend's mug left behind in my room; I carry these things with me everywhere. Home is, for me, where my things are. I have learned that I cannot and do not have the people I love around me all the time, and the constant change in where I have lived has meant that I have no roots anywhere physical. So, I carry my home with me wherever I go. Home is not a place, but a feeling, and this is something that many expat children learn early on. Whatever I can do to bring about that feeling is enough for me.

What impact has expatriation had on your life?

As I mentioned, I spent a lot of my life living in Beijing. I went to the same school, and lived in the same house for almost 10 years. Compared to many expat children, this was a relatively stable life. However, I felt the effects of expatriation keenly all the same: friends moved in and out of my life every couple of years, moving from place to place. I was constantly having to say goodbye to people in my life. I also felt removed from my extended family. With my mum's family still in Hong Kong, and my dad's at first in the UK, then Belgium, and now Australia, I never got the experience of having a big family the way I would have liked.

This is something that many of my expatriate friends have mentioned too. The process of constantly saying goodbye, and feeling estranged from family members is a harsh one. I believe that it is the most painful consequence of being an expatriate. Especially as a child, growing up was harder, feeling slightly unstable the whole time, knowing that at any moment the life I knew could be swept out from under my feet – my friends could leave, or I would. This was never a question of "if" but of "when." Luckily for me, I never isolated myself, or felt that I couldn't make strong connections with people because of a fear that I would lose them. This is, however, a common experience with expat children, and I have seen it in many of my expat friends.

However, despite the few negative impacts, I am so glad to have been an expat. Expatriation has enabled me to become the person that I am; open-minded, inclusive, adaptable and patient. The constant change that I have experienced and feared has caused far more benefits than problems for me. I have seen this most clearly in the past year or two, during the COVID-19 pandemic. During this time, the entire world population has been thrown into complete disarray – nothing is certain and everyone feels unstable (to different degrees, of course). I am very lucky to have the privileged life I do, in that COVID-19 has not devastated my life the way it has with many others my age specifically. I have had access to education (online) and communication with my friends the whole time. This is a privilege I know not everyone has had, and for that I am incredibly grateful.

The majority of my friends, similarly advantaged, have had similar experiences to me. However, the different ways in which my expat friends and I processed the pandemic and its subsequent effects are telling; my non-expat friends were constantly stressed, they felt completely at loss without the usual stability and order of their lives. Not knowing when things were going to happen put them in a position they had never experienced before, but with which expats are familiar: uncertainty.

As expats, we have to learn to take situations and feelings and make the best of them, and uncertainty is one of those. I have learnt to be patient amidst complete insecurity, and to engineer out of it something worthwhile. My friends, having never faced such an obstacle, were not able to do this. They were completely paralyzed with anxiety in this new world, and I managed to keep moving in it. This was because, and only because, I am adaptable, and I make situations work for me. All of my expat friends are the same, and this has just proved how significantly expatriation has benefited our lives. We are prepared for anything, and this will help us at every obstacle going forward.

Do you ever feel envious of kids who never moved? Why?

I will admit that in the past, I used to be incredibly jealous of my non-expat friends. Many of my friends at boarding school have never moved house, let alone country. They know everyone in their local village, have old marks on the kitchen door to track their heights as they grew, and can paint their walls whatever color they'd like, because they don't have to worry about what happens when the lease runs out. This seemed at first like a dream to me. However, I have come to realize that I would not trade my expatriate life for anything, and while I have always wondered what a stable home would be like, it is no longer something I wish for.

One thing that I have found is that almost all of my closest friends are expatriates, even at boarding school. We find each other wherever we go. I almost always click better with expats than anyone else, and we not only find common ground in our experiences, but in our values. My boyfriend and many of my best friends at school are expats. I have found that expats tend to be more open-minded, welcoming and inclusive than non-expats. Of course, there are exceptions and this is by no means applicable to everyone, but it is what I have found. Expats are more likely to stick around and help new kids, to make the effort to help people who need them. They are less likely to judge, and more likely to forgive. They are patient, and above all, they are independent.

Anyone can have these traits, of course, but the experiences of an expat home develops them faster and stronger: constantly having new kids at school (or being the new kid) makes you kind and welcoming. Being exposed to people of all different backgrounds and cultures makes you open-minded, accepting, and less judgmental. Knowing that time is precious makes you recognize the relative importance of different issues, and makes you forgiving when you need to be. Finally, having to be there for yourself in times of change makes you independent and strong. These are the people that I am drawn to, and are drawn to me. Expatriation makes kids wonderful people, and teaches them skills that others take years to develop. Being an expat made me a person that I am proud of, and

I am grateful for all the experiences that enabled this for me.

While initially I felt envious of kids who had never moved, I no longer feel that way, because I know that without expatriation, I would not be half the person I am today.

What do you wish your parents had done more of, or what did they do right?

As I mentioned before, I am incredibly grateful for the life that I have. My parents have given me fantastic opportunities and I could not thank them more for everything they have done. With regards to our lives as expats, the most important thing has always been having a circle of friends. Being away from family, you have to make your own and my parents have always done this. They made friends that became like aunts and uncles to me, and whose children I have grown up with. While of course my parents' friendships were more for their benefit, not mine, I still found that I really appreciated having a healthy and supportive environment around me, and the relationships that my parents maintained made this possible.

If there was one thing you wanted to share with parents who will have expat children, what would it be?

To parents who will have expat children, it is important to understand that it will not always be easy. This nomadic way of life is not conventional, and as a result it raises unconventional people – remarkable people. People who understand the world. Money cannot buy the education that being an expat provides. However, to decide to introduce your children into a life of constant change, to ask them to get used to saying goodbye, to being uprooted, and to sometimes feeling lonely, is a big choice to make.

I asked some of my expat friends to think about this question too, and we all said similar things. For a parent who will have expat children, you should:

- Make sure that you and your child have good communication.

For every parent-child relationship, communication is important, but in an expat situation this is even more essential. The emotions that come with the expat life are overwhelming, and to get through them your child will need your help. They will need to feel like they can come to you and talk to you about anything, and you need to be there when they do. Equally, this means that you need to be honest and open with them, and they will follow.

- Get yourself and your child involved in as many activities and groups as you can.

I mentioned that my parents have always had many friends. This is because they made sure to get involved in groups and societies themselves and find them. For me, these relationships were incredibly important.

Similarly, you need to get your kids involved in groups too. Moving from place to place, it becomes disheartening making friends knowing you will leave them, or vice versa. Being around different groups of people all the time is a good way to fight this, as is encouraging hobbies and activities that make them happy. There are always plenty of options in expat communities for this kind of thing, so make sure you keep it in mind.

And finally, above all, to any parent or child – do not let yourself waste this opportunity. Being an expatriate gives you access to unique experiences that can change your life and give you the tools you need to be exceptional – but only if you let them.

I would like to thank Imi for being so honest and transparent with us and for putting so much energy into her reflection. I hope that by sharing this story, it will help to answer those of you who are now considering whether or not to raise your children in an expatriate environment.

Reflections...

To help identify what is important for you to know about third culture kids, I invite you to reflect on these questions:

- What experience do you have with a third culture kid situation?

- What comes to mind hearing Imogen's story?

- Considering your own life experience, what would your children gain from being raised as expatriates?

CHAPTER

ELEVEN

Being happy is a state of mind

Your experience will make you believe in yourself...

In my book, I have talked a lot about encounters; about their importance and their richness. Despite the significance of interacting with others, I still believe that the most important encounter I have had has been the encounter with *myself.*

Through my adventures, I have become aware of my strengths and the skills I had to develop in order to enjoy my life to the fullest. Little by little the successes and satisfactions I have had in my experience have accumulated, and my self-confidence has allowed me to create my true identity.

Creating our identity in expatriation is important for us women and wives. It is our way of settling into our new life and being recognized as our true self, to be addressed as "your name" not as "Mrs... wife of..." or the "trailing spouse."

At the beginning of the expatriation, two attitudes are particularly necessary: resilience and flexibility. Very quickly, we all develop our own strengths and, above all, we discover more and more competencies. The opportunities we have to develop these skills will make us unique and desirable in the working world amongst other life experiences.

If I think for example of partners who wish to find a job during their expatriation abroad, the general skills found during the expatriation process, often taken for granted, could suddenly highlight the uniqueness of the individual to a potential employer.

Dealing with your frustrations...

Expatriation is also about learning to deal with our frustrations. We soon come to realize that no destination is perfect. However, for the purposes of remaining positive and sane, we learn to become peaceful in a wider range of circumstances.

Since during our postings we are mainly mixing with other cultures, it is really important to understand the locals, choose our battles and avoid conflicts. Remember, it really depends on you and what you decide to do there that will make the experience successful or not. It is definitely a question of personal perspective.

I have always been curious and positive and like to be on the move. I have always sought to meet people but it has also been important for me to do something that interests me, that energizes me, that makes me feel responsible and above all that gives me satisfaction. Moreover, I admit that if a situation bores me, I move on to something that gives me more energy and makes me happier. I think it's also interesting to observe how prejudices and preconceived ideas about oneself can disappear during expatriation experiences and leave a space open for a new self.

In every country I have lived in, I have always been amazed by the number of women who have succeeded in developing passions and businesses because they have let their inspiration and courage speak for themselves. Many of them have left a real mark on the countries in which they have lived. Some of them have also taken their businesses with them and continue to run their careers, their businesses, wherever they are.

It is always with great admiration and pleasure that I see so many women flourish around me during their expatriation. I really want to take a moment to pay tribute to all these extraordinary women who have put so much energy, love and passion into what they believe in. They have overcome various challenges to make their dream a reality.

There is even a new term for these amazing women: they are "Womanpreneur."

Painters, writers, event planners, jewelry designers, guides, stylists, I would have liked to name them all, but there are so many that I can only congratulate them in this book and express my admiration.

Courage...

I think it is important to talk about this incredible strength that all of us expatriate women have within us. If at the beginning of the expatriation this strength propelled us in our new life, I want to believe that with time, courage becomes the driving force of our lives, and empowers us to make new decisions.

Even when surrounded by friends and family, it is true that women often start their expatriate lives with many moments of loneliness. This is an obstacle that often requires a good dose of courage for a woman to take charge and use her resources to immerse herself in her new environment.

On a personal level, my life path has asked me to take more and more responsibility for myself and my life. I acknowledge how much I have evolved as an individual. A first observation would be that expat life has always required a lot of commitment, flexibility, creativity and tolerance from myself. Indirectly, I was always stimulated to make choices: to challenge myself and decide what I was going to do next to use my time in the best way I could in my new environment.

As I mentioned before, in expatriation one also experiences a great paradox with the concept of time passing. Depending on the life you choose, professional or not, in absolute terms, you can have a lot of time for yourself to do what you want. On the other hand, your time is also counted because the postings are often time-limited.

You don't always have time to think and evaluate, so time suddenly becomes precious. I am constantly reminded to ask myself what would empower me, what would fulfill me in the future and make me happy. Unconsciously, I was always waiting impatiently for the "right thing" to come to me – the passion, the unique opportunity that I would master in each particular country. In the meantime, life moves on and the roles we take on multiply too. Expatriate partners should be recognized for their own individual worth!

Alex has always been great at this. He has always supported me in my projects and motivated me in everything I have undertaken. Having his confidence has surely been the key to my success and happiness. Feeling the positive energy around you can only push you forward and bring out the best in you. I will always remember this book project that happened very quickly and completely by chance.

While I had always wanted to write about my expatriate years so that my children would know what we had experienced, I had never thought of sharing my life experience publicly. It was really when I came across Emilia's story in her book, *It's your life*, that I realized that it would be with Mindy, a book coach, that I could consider this project. It all clicked, everything went very fast, the pieces of the puzzle came together. I remembered what my friends often tell me, that my life as a serial expat could really inspire other women. All of a sudden, I felt like listening to them and undertaking this project by combining my story and my job.

As soon as I had done my initial research, I spoke to Alex who thought it was a great idea. I was speechless! He immediately believed in me and above all he encouraged me to pursue my project from A to Z. A project that I must say was quite fast, since it took exactly 12 weeks from the moment I put my first word on paper to sending off the manuscript.

One life, multiple roles...

For example, if I look at my roles, along with being an expat partner, I am a wife, a mother, an employer, a friend, a life coach, a host for my family and friends, a painter and now even an author! Each of these roles is important to me because they define me as a person. I chose them, they fulfill me, they energize me and they inspire me.

My role as a wife...

I left Geneva 25 years ago, being Alex's girlfriend. This year we are celebrating 21 years of marriage. Besides love and respect, there are several key factors to this longevity: the excitement of constant newness, the common desire to continue discovering the world and sharing every moment together. The willingness to take risks together and be ready to assume the consequences together. Keeping in mind the importance of exchanging and communicating to help each other to do better than if we were alone. We share the same vision: our vision, our common dreams, as well as our personal ambitions. We respect and support each other's choices. We know that what we are building today will help us to realize our dream of tomorrow and prepare our future. Our constant commitment to each other and our lives maintains a kind of permanent balance.

We respect each other's roles, ambition and responsibilities while keeping our family as our priority. Our common goal is for each member of the family to unleash their full potential and be happy.

My role as a mother...

For expatriate parents who have children at school, I think you will sympathize with me when I say that at the time of the announcement of a transfer, one of the first concerns is which school we will enroll our children in. No matter if the children are in kindergarten or in high school, it is an anxious process.

I remember when we returned to Mexico after our exploratory trip to the Philippines; I had found neither a house to my liking, nor space for my kids in the school I wanted. I was obviously disappointed and upset. For me, there was only one option for my children's education: the International School Manila (ISM).

It is not uncommon for international companies not to have priority access to the school of your choice. This is what happened to us when we arrived in Manila. The company my husband works for did not have a seat in the international school in Manila because Alex's predecessor had enrolled his children in the British School and because of our passports, our family did not have access to that school. The company in the Philippines could not guarantee us a place in any school, a new challenge we had to face.

While in Mexico, I used to go to my Pilates classes and I regularly met the same people there. Two Tuesdays in a row I ended up with a woman who told me she had a lovely Mexican friend who had moved to Manila. The first week I took her friend's name, Lupita, and thought I would call her when I got there, and then the second week, finding these encounters strangely coincidental, I felt like getting in touch with Lupita. I remember, the movers were starting to pack up my house and I organically offered to Lupita to take advantage of my move if she had something she would like me to bring from Mexico to Manila. It happened that she had just received a dinner set from her children and was very keen to have it with her. To show her gratitude, she generously offered to return the favor and asked me if she could help me with anything special in Manila. As a joke and literally having nothing else in mind, I wrote to her in a rush: "a house and a school!" knowing full well that my answer was an unrealistic request.

Two days later, Lupita answered me by asking in which school I wanted to enroll my children, I told her my wish, and her husband happened to be on the board of directors of ISM. My children were added to the waiting list, and as soon as there was space, they were accepted. I was relieved, the children would be in what I thought was the best school for them, given their background. From this point, my transition period became much less psychologically stressful.

As I mentioned before, parents can only be happy when their children find a routine, when they see them reassured, start to make friends and become happy in their new environment.

My role as a friend...

In expatriation, the women who are already in the country often welcome the newcomers in their turn. In Brazil, I was in Curitiba for a few months when Fernanda first arrived. I remember that I immediately went up to this Argentinean mother, who was accompanying her little Lara to school. Lara was going to join Constantin's class.

Fernanda quickly became like a sister to me. Right away she was very present and engaged. Geographically, Brazil is really far from Europe, even the seasons are opposite. It was a time in my life when I felt far away and really out of place from my friends and family and I needed a close friend by my side.

It was also during that period that I got pregnant with Angelina. My sensitivity as a young mother and pregnant woman was definitely the perfect combination to welcome such a genuine and sincere friendship into my life. Fernanda also had little Lisa who was a few months old. Fernanda was very dynamic, always caring, generous, funny, positive, the kind of friend you dream of wherever you are in the world! At the same time, Constantin and Lara also developed their friendship, they became inseparable despite their young age at only three years old. Inevitably, our two families became very close and we have enjoyed many wonderful years of friendship in Brazil and elsewhere. As it happened, our expatriate mission in Brazil ended around the same time, and then we went to visit them in Costa Rica and Guatemala, and they met us in Mexico.

This is an example of the kind of friendships that I hope will never end; Fernanda and her beautiful family will always be in our hearts.

Ambitious and active women...

No matter the destination, I always put a priority on staying connected with myself and my values. When I was younger I never self-reflected on my way of thinking and functioning. I believe I can say today that I am attracted to the unknown and to challenges. Whenever a curiosity arises in me, I look for the solution to satisfy it. Being a problem solver is also part of my DNA – I enjoy it. Finding solutions to mine and others' problems is what drives me. I have always let myself dream and listened to myself, but I've also had to push myself to overcome my fears and ignore my inner voice that told me I would not be able to achieve them.

Over time, my fear of failure gradually faded away and was replaced by the satisfaction of having achieved my dreams, and the knowledge that I could continue to do so. The more I took risks and fulfilled myself, the more my negative voice faded away to make room for a positive and inspiring inner voice.

Being more isolated has given me the chance to feel a little less judged by my family and friends. I have felt less in the spotlight, and thus free to try new things, to take more risks. Today, the way others look at me does not have the same impact on me. If at the time I equated success with perfection, (a very subjective notion) today I accept imperfection and I define my success according to my personal requirements, objectives and satisfaction.

This discovery about myself has given me access to a range of opportunities that I never thought were available to me. We all have beliefs that we need to "discreate" in order to move forward in life.

This awareness has given me more self-confidence, made me naturally more authentic in my relationships with people and with myself. No longer worrying about other people's opinions gives me the freedom to be whole.

My role as an author...

The exercise of writing this book was not only an important writing exercise but also a new personal development exercise and eventually a new goal: to take my coaching to the next level.

By choosing to write this book, I also gave myself the chance to choose a communication tool that allows me to connect with other women who also want to progress, transform and grow to achieve their dreams by working on their skills, values and strengths.

This project required courage and also a good support structure. I have had invaluable support from Mindy. As a great coach, Mindy believed in me, and being a coach myself, I knew that with the help of a guide and my own will to get there, I could achieve the desired outcome.

If you are reading this book, it is because it has been published, the project has come to fruition, and you can imagine my joy at having achieved it!

Reflections...

To help you think about yourself, I invite you to reflect on these questions:

- What ambitions do you have?

- What would you like to do if you had more time?

- What would you like to do if you were given a new start?

CHAPTER

TWELVE

The freedom of the expat life is a gift

Today, I can truly thank life for this wonderful gift it has given me: living an expat life with my better half, Alex. I also want to acknowledge that if we consider our expat life as a gift, it is because Alex and I are a real team, completely aligned with our choices and that this adventure is so far a real success for both of us as a couple and as a family.

I was open to the opportunities of expatriation at the time because it came at the right time in my personal life, and for us as a couple. We were both looking for exciting life experiences and had just enough time together to be willing to share this first journey with each other.

Honored by this gift, I wanted to thank the world from the start by adopting a positive and open attitude which would allow me to live this adventure fully. I decided to be open to all the surprises and novelties in my expat life, and to let the story come to me without overthinking.

Looking at the choice as a growing experience...

Our choices as global nomads have often been stressful, particularly when important decisions have had to be made quickly. Also, the options available to us are themselves unfamiliar. We have often found ourselves in environments that are very different from those in which we grew up and in the face of this unfamiliarity, our choices have felt to have greater consequences.

For example, unless you have been an expatriate child yourself, it is rare to be familiar with the different curriculum offered by the schools our children will attend. By choosing a certain school curriculum among others, you are already unconsciously influencing their choice in their further education.

Another example is your choice of destinations. At the end of a mission, you decide whether to renew the experience or not, in a country that is imposed on you or one of your choosing. Whatever your decision may be, you will influence your future and that of your family.

Personally, these choices have led me to questions and personal reflections that often fascinate me. They are the essence of my personal drive. I like to be challenged and empowered, I feel alive!

I like to have choices, and they do not scare me anymore. I know that I will not always make the best choices for myself or my family, but I have learned to accept the risks I take, and their consequences. I have learned to accept failure as a constructive element that allows me to grow and evolve.

Open to new experiences...

By going abroad, we inevitably open up to other cultures. Families who go abroad with children also offer them a unique experience, an opening to others and even a school of humility and integration. Our adventures can really take us from laughter to tears, to special adventures, to living an exceptional life.

However, I think that the nomadic life is really a life that you choose. Even if you lived it as a child with your parents, it is important to respect the fact that this life is more difficult in terms of adaptation for some people than for others. I remember listening to a TCK expert who was invited to a conference on expatriation at the International School Manila. She explained that in the same family of expatriate siblings, each child had their own vision of their future. Not all children who have experienced expatriation automatically choose an expatriate life with their future family. They often decide to settle in a city of their choice and do not think about moving.

However, being an expat does not mean that we deny or abandon our roots. Being open to new experiences does not take away from our need for a grounded life, a home. Expatriate packages often include a return trip to our home country or financial compensation that enables us to travel to a country of our choice. These returns are an invitation to reconnect with family and friends and to share with our children the traditions of our childhood. For my children, who have never lived in Switzerland or Austria, by choice they have defined two places that they consider their home. Two places to which they are particularly attached, two places in which they have created special memories, a place to reconnect with a feeling of home. The first is our family chalet in Austria and the second is a house on the Mexican coast that we built in the second year of our stay in Mexico.

In Austria, this home is where we celebrate Christmas every other year and spend a few weeks every summer.

My in-laws meet us there, and the children have their own rooms. They enjoy fishing in the river, riding horses and having lunch in the traditional mountain pastures. It is also a place where we like to invite my family and our friends known in expatriation or even before.

When we arrived in Mexico, we were quickly charmed by the country and its culture. It has always been a dream of ours to build a house by the sea. In Mexico we had the opportunity to do so and we had the courage to go for it. The construction of this house is definitely one of the highlights of our expat life. From the choice of land to the handover of the house, the children were involved in the whole process. Both Constantin and Angelina have seen how much we have been personally involved in making the house a dream for our whole family. We were lucky to build "Casa en las Rocas" with Enrique Zozaya, an extremely kind, discreet and humble architect who worked with all our wishes and transformed them in a perfect way to make this house a stunning dream house.

As a family, we took the time to source materials and resources in Mexico. Each room has its own theme and color, my children saw me paint each painting, create the cushions, the bedside lamps and some artworks strewn around the house.

For my children, this house represents their childhood, a house in which we receive our family and friends from Mexico and elsewhere in the world. This house has enabled our children to also receive guests in their own home. Even today, although we live far away from Mexico, we return there as often as possible. Christmas 2019, just before the

COVID-19 pandemic, we were all together, 19 cousins, brothers, sisters and grandparents – a lifetime memory for all of us.

A general observation I have made during my expatriate years is that the happiest people I have met are those who are always shaking up their routine with new and different experiences. This goes to show how significant it is to have many facets to your life – to take on new experiences, to challenge and grow. However, I feel you should always remember your roots and home; it will inevitably make you a happier person.

A passion...

One of my biggest regrets is that I never made a journal to recount all my memories. At the time, I always thought I would never forget, but today, looking back, I realize that in some countries it was almost every day that I experienced extraordinary situations; what I was used to seeing, hearing, smelling, touching, tasting. My senses were constantly stimulated! Fortunately, I always liked to make photo albums which serve as visual diaries of our adventures.

The way I live my expat experiences has also evolved. If at the beginning of my expatriate life, I was scattered and sought to embrace all opportunities, adventures and experiences to broaden my horizons and those of my family, over the years, I have refined my choices to focus on certain areas that I find fulfilling and interesting.

I believe it is the same for each of us; at our own pace, given the means, we all discover sooner rather than later what makes us happy, or, for the luckiest, passionate!

For Constantin he discovered karting and racing at the age of 10. Very soon, this sport became his passion and he chose to invest himself 100% in it. To reach his dreams and goals, he made a choice that requires a lot of personal organization (time management), personal discipline and physical effort (Constantin also had to impose a strict diet to reach a certain weight and maintain it).

Constantin had to learn to manage his sport, his studies, his trips abroad and above all his emotions. To flourish, he had to find his balance between his sport, mental stimulation, and social interaction. His father was his best coach and an extremely close relationship developed between the two of them. Constantin has been so successful in the last seven years of karting, and this is undoubtedly due to the important decisions he has made for himself, his perseverance and his commitment.

Following and accompanying Constantin in his passion was also an important family decision. We had to consider all the solutions so that Alex could find his balance between the week traveling for his work, the weekends with his son on the circuits and time for his daughter and his wife. Alex decided he could do it, we trusted him and we all made the effort to help Constantin realize his dream. It took all four of us to step up, to venture out of our comfort zones again, to discover that we were able to handle these new situations and to all accompany Constantin in his magnificent successes!

I believe that there is no age to live one's passion. I have always lived the concept of expatriation with passion and my greatest desire is to share it with you. To all the expat women or future expats for whom my experiences resonate, to all who want to go further in their journey:

One life, live it!

Everything is going to be alright!

Be kind to yourself, the world is yours!

REFLECTIONS

ABOUT THE AUTHOR

Florence Reisch-Gentinetta is a serial expat. Originally from Switzerland, she has lived around the world for the last 25 years with her Austrian husband and their two third culture kids.

Wherever she lived, Florence always looked for opportunities to reinvent herself. Being creative and flexible, she kept on being busy, happy and living a fulfilled exciting life.

Her empathy for people and her curiosity about the world led her to a very unique expatriation experience that she wanted to share with you.

Florence is a bilingual advanced certified life coach (International Coaching Federation ICF) with a special focus on expatriates. Passionate about people and how they respond to their emotions and life changes, she supports women and third culture kids who want to better understand themselves, overcome their fears, gain confidence and unleash their full potential.

Dubai is her home for now but she works internationally. If you would like to contact her, she would love to hear from you at www.coachingwiththeflo.com

Made in United States
North Haven, CT
18 April 2023